Advance Praise for *Business Is Dead*

"Pop culture is a very broad realm and approaching the topic of entrepreneurship within this area could be overwhelming. I really appreciate the way author Neil A. Cohen approached the subject. By choosing just one pop culture phenom to analyze, as he did with *The Walking Dead*, he provided a really well-crafted narrative that can be applied to any fan focused entrepreneurial venture."
—Lance Fensterman, President, ReedPOP Global

✧

"Fandom is a complex subject to cover, and like anything complicated in life, there are nuances. I love that you are writing about fantrepreneurs. I am fascinated by it. I can't wait to read it and I am proud to be a small part of it."
—Jay Bonansinga, Author, *The Walking Dead* Woodbury series

Also by Neil A. Cohen

Exit Zero Zombie trilogy

Exit Zero
Nuke Jersey
Zombie Democracy

BUSINESS IS DEAD

RESURRECTING ENTREPRENEURSHIP
THROUGH THE FAN-FOCUSED VENTURE

Neil A. Cohen, M.B.A. D.O.A.

PERMUTED
PRESS

A PERMUTED PRESS BOOK
ISBN: 978-1-68261-886-8
ISBN (eBook): 978-1-68261-887-5

Business Is Dead:
Resurrecting Entrepreneurship Through the Fan-Focused Venture
© 2019 by Neil A. Cohen, M.B.A. D.O.A.
All Rights Reserved

Cover art by Jomel Cequina

PERMUTED
PRESS

Permuted Press, LLC
New York • Nashville
permutedpress.com

Published in the United States of America

TABLE OF CONTENTS

INTRODUCTION

I have always been a fan of entrepreneurs, and there have been countless success stories attributed to them. Many have become household names, such as Michael Dell, Bill Gates and Oprah. When I decided to write about fantrepreneurs, I wanted to reach out to those whose who have reached a level of success that their names would also be known, at least within the pop culture fandom community. Well, if anyone knows, and is known by, pop culture fandom it's Lance Fensterman, founder and president of ReedPOP, a brand known globally for their pop culture-inspired events and merchandise. I reached out to the ReedPOP company in hopes of getting a message passed along to the corporation's president asking for his insights into the fandom-inspired entrepreneurial venture. Knowing this was a large organization with a global presence, I assumed my chances were slim to none. At best, I thought I would get hold of someone within their public relations division who would give me a canned response to interview requests. I was surprised at how quickly his team responded and within one day, I was corresponding with Mr. Fensterman via email, as he was, at the time, overseas. The promptness of their response to my request demonstrated that firm's outstanding customer care and support of the fandom community.

"The topic of fantrepreneurship is something that I have been involved with for many years and not even realized there was a term for it. Fantrepreneurs are reinventing the way to approach a new business or to turn around an existing business that may be struggling. The fantrepreneur sector is being led by creative, enthusiastic, highly innovative, and entrepreneurial people in a wide array of industries." Lance continued. "When I formed ReedPOP as a division within Reed Exhibitions back in 2005, I did so to create a pure pop culture event division. By 2018 ReedPOP was hosting forty-four fan-focused events across eleven countries."

ReedPOP is probably best known for the NYC Comic-Con, a massive celebration of all things both mainstream and counter-culture.

CHAPTER ONE

JOINING THE HORDE

This is not a book about *The Walking Dead*. Sorry to disappoint you if you thought it was, and no, you can't have your money back. This is also not a book about traditional entrepreneurship, as I will not cover the mechanics of how to run your small business, manage your corporate finances, and maneuver through the associated tax and legal requirements of starting and running your own business. There are thousands of business books on those topics. Pick any one you like. But be warned, they are all boring and none contain zombies.

I am not kidding, search Amazon for books on entrepreneurship. Go ahead, I will wait. I told you, there were over forty thousand results. Now don't ever doubt me again!

This book is about the fantrepreneur. At the time of writing this, do you know how many books are listed on the topic of the fantrepreneur? Zero! When entrepreneurs identify a space where no one is providing a product or service, they move quickly to fill it.

While term "entrepreneur" has been around for over two hundred years, defining individuals who undertake some form of business venture—generally without any guarantee of profit or success—the term "fantrepreneur" has only been around for a brief time. Fantrepreneurship describes businesses that are started by fans, for fans. These are entrepreneurs who are not primarily driven by the potential for financial profit, or any profit in philanthropic endeavors, but those who crave both involvement within their favorite genre along with affiliation with fellow fans. Later, I will delve deeper into the research and origin story of the term "fantrepreneur."

Even within an industry as micro-focused as pop culture fandom, there lie delineations of tastes, interests, and consumer habits so vast, I could not hope to tackle the full spectrum in a single book. So why am I focusing this book on fandom of *The Walking Dead?* Because that is where I formed my first fantrepreneurial venture and it is an area I have become both involved and fascinated with for the past several years.

It would seem antithetical to launch my first entrepreneurship with *The Walking Dead* as its foundation. After all, this is a genre that involves such depressing and (to many) off-putting topics—such as the near end to humanity, a spreading pandemic that causes the dead to rise and become shambling cannibalistic shells of the friends and family they once were, and a world where the living can become psychopathic strongmen...or worse. Why would people want to focus on the most horrifically imagined catastrophic event in all recorded human history, which would be the *end* of recorded human history? Wouldn't an entrepreneur want to align their new business venture with a pop culture genre that is less dark, more positive, uplifting and hope-inspiring?

The definitive answer to that question is...probably. But hey, most people spend their life avoiding the dark route to a destination. Where is the fun and challenge in that?

We all need an escape plan from the stresses of life. My mental escape always included books, films, and television shows with a zombie apocalypse theme. I do not know why I chose that particular niche of fandom, I am sure many professional psychologists and arm-chair analysts would have their opinions. But it was what it was. I was not a fan of the traditional horror genre in general—the slasher films, the jump-scare films. I was only interested in the storyline of a book or film if it fell into my own personal "Goldilocks Zone", which is a term used for describing the exact mixture of elements to support life, though my zone had two elements; zombies and the apocalypse. My fascination with zombies first started from an obsessive fear of them during childhood. I began watching zombie movies way too early, and I really do believe that is where it all started. I remember my sister and her friends letting me join them while watching *Children Shouldn't Play with Dead Things* in the early 1970s. Later, I saw just the TV commercial for the movie *Dawn of the Dead* and did not sleep for a week. The zombies had invaded my psyche and there was no purging them.

Zombies touch on so many fears. The fear of death and sickness, the fear of not being able to protect your loved ones. The fear of societal collapse and the fragility of civilization. I faced my fear by embracing that which I was most afraid of. As Aristotle once said, "nature abhors a vacuum," and once I conquered one fear, others flooded in. Now I'm riddled with much more normal fears, like the falling economy or my rising cholesterol level. I miss those simpler times when my greatest anxieties were centered around flesh-eating, reanimated cadavers.

At the time, my obsession was truly a niche interest. There were few sources of new material to get my fix, other than the occasional cultish movie or small publisher. As such, I assumed I was one of a very few who enjoyed this content. After all, if zombies were a mainstream taste, there would be a plethora of TV shows, books, and movies about them. But there weren't, so I kept my obsession to myself. I did not want to be viewed as an outlier. I did not even share my interest with my social media friends. Back in the '80s, my social media circle consisted of my friends whom I had grown up with, and our social media platform was the plastic, wall-mounted, rotary phone in our kitchen. I recall when they first introduced conference calling, which allowed you to bring as many as three people together into a single phone conversation. Amazing, you could communicate to two people, over the air, at once. It was like a podcast, only with at least two people listening.... *It's a joke, people!* I love my podcasting friends.

When *The Walking Dead* TV series first premiered in 2010 and over five million viewers tuned in, I realized I was not alone in my fandom of the zombie genre. I loved *The Walking Dead's* (*TWD*) storyline, but I felt I had a different take on how the zombie pandemic could begin and how the people, business, and government would manage the situation. I started writing short stories about average people and how they would react to the beginning of the zombie outbreak—i.e., all the stuff that was happening while Rick was in a coma during *TWD*. I continued writing these stories, loosely weaving them into an overarching narrative, for the next couple years without any plan on what to do with them. By the time the fourth season of *TWD* premiered and over sixteen million viewers tuned in, I knew this was not a fad. Turned out, there was a market out there hungry for this type of entertainment, with fans voracious in consuming anything that fit this genre. I just needed to figure out what I could provide to meet this unmet undead desire.

I knew that if I could identify that one product or service that would attract *TWD*'s fanbase, I could enter this market. I saw their gnashing teeth, I felt their hunger, I just needed to feed them without sacrificing myself or my life savings while doing so. I decided to form an LLC and combine all my short stories into a trilogy of zombie novels. That was my way to contribute my own ideas and vision to the ever-growing canon of cannibalistic artistry.

Before then, I had never wanted to write a book. I had rarely ever wanted to read a book. But I was determined that becoming an author and selling my own books was my entrepreneurial path forward. So, I had to learn two things quickly. How do I write a book, and how do I sell it?

I had an MBA and nearly three decades of both domestic and international business development experience under my belt, yet I had never started or run my own endeavor. I had my passion, I had my product idea, I just needed to find the way forward. As it's easier to dig a grave in already tilled soil, I set out to talk to as many people as I could who were already fantrepreneurs focused on either *TWD* or the zombie/horror genre in general.

These are the stories of just a few artists, philanthropists, and entrepreneurs that began their journey with inspiration from their fandom of *TWD* franchise. Each person in this book has carved out a niche for themselves. Each forged their own paths, had their own successes and failures, found a way to stand out within a crowded marketplace, and in some cases, created an entirely new market.

There are many types of fantrepreneurs. Those that focus on comic books and superheroes, those that focus on sports teams, those that focus on television and movies. I want to focus on just one specific grouping of fandom—a subset segmentation to the fourth power:

- Fandom genre = Horror (Subset)
- Horror genre = Apocalyptic (Sub-subset)

- Apocalyptic genre = Zombie (Sub-sub-subset)
- Zombie series of choice = *The Walking Dead* (Sub-sub-sub-subset)

I call this very slim slice of the fantrepreneur pie chart the *deadtrepreneur*. I would have called it the more easily pronounceable *dead*icated, but that term was taken to describe fandom of the Grateful Dead. Damn hippies.

I will not drill down further into the deeper-level delineations of the zombie dogma, such as the argument that the term "zombie" should only refer to the re-animated dead and not to infected living, or the even more controversial "fast-moving zombies" versus "slow-moving zombies" debate. I know passions can run hot on those topics. Let keep things friendly here. No arguments and please don't flame me on Twitter. I have already pissed off the damn hippies. Sheesh!

So how do I know there is even an audience for a topic this micro-focused? Because I have spoken to them. Lots of them. For the nearly half-dozen years I have been selling my books at horror and zombie cons, I have taken any downtime I have at events to visit the other vendors, learn why they chose to enter this market, why they create, draw, paint, sculpt, build, photograph, create cosplay costumes, and even bake cookies as tributes to *TWD*. There was no one I did not find interesting.

Is there really a "word" fantrepreneur? No, it is a mash up of words, like *Brangelina*, *sexting* or *bromance*. For the purposes of this book, I was going to refer to them as deadtrepreneurs, because I am so clever. But I won't. That was a bad idea. Not "Hershel keeping his dead-yet-hungry family in the barn next door" level of bad idea, but a bad idea just the same. While this book will focus on those that started their fan-based business venture ignited by their *TWD* fandom, this book is for all fandoms. So, let's stick with the established term: fantrepreneur.

So, as the word *deadtrepreneur* is led outside towards a waiting bullet and a shallow grave, we can forget all this ugliness occurred and continue onward.

I am sorry you had to bear witness to that, but sometimes observing an author's process is enlightening. Now, I am sure there will be people unhappy with the term *fantrepreneur* as well. But suck it up, buttercup. There is a new sheriff in town, and his name is Fantrepreneur.

CHAPTER TWO

MY OWN SHAMBLE TOWARDS ~~DEADTREPRENEUR~~ FANTREPRENEUR

Around 2013, I began submitting my aforementioned zombie book concepts to publishers. I had no idea what I was doing, had no understanding of the publishing world and no fan base. The publishers rightfully told me to go jump in a shallow grave.

So, I went the self-publishing route. I began promoting it at small comic and pop culture cons, and had moderate success based on creating a fun atmosphere around purchasing the book. I would set up an elaborate display at each show that resembled a prison overrun by zombies. I had lots of props such as gas masks, hazmat suits, and faux weapons to draw people over. In my book, I had cool graphics throughout to entice the comic-book buyer. I tracked my book sales and sent those posted sales numbers off to the same publishers that had rejected me. While they were not overwhelmed by my grammatical skills, they saw I could craft an original story and, just as importantly, they could count on me to promote and sell my own books. By the end of 2015, the first book was complete and set to be released the following year. I was far along in the writing process of the subsequent two books, and knowing I now had a product line, it was time to flesh out my business plan. I set out to expand the potential market in which to sell, since I had already gone the comic-con route and determined that I needed to reach a broader customer base.

I began attending local publishing events, writer's conferences, and small press expos that featured independent authors and illustrators of graphic novels. This was a very different audience than I had experienced at generic comic cons, one that would require a different type of sales approach than I had been using.

Granted, I was a born salesman. My first paid job was while in grade school. A friend's father paid us to run through store parking lots and put flyers for his small business on car windshields. He noticed that instead of anonymously placing the flyer, I would gravitate towards the direct approach, walking up to shoppers and asking them to take the flyers. He began paying me more to stand by the exits and get people to take the flyers. I worked on several pitches that would make the adults laugh and take the leaflet. My friend was jealous, since his father was putting more focus on me than his son. By the end of the summer, I lost my friend but made fifty bucks. The corporate climb to wealth can be ruthless and isolating, even at ten years old.

In college, I began working weekends in New York City as a street vendor. I would go to the wholesale district downtown and buy bulk novelties such as plastic flowers or sunglasses that lit up. We called them "tchotchkes," which I believe is an ancient Yiddish phrase for cheap crap. I would walk around the tourist areas of Times Square and Rockefeller Center with the items stuck into a foam display and an extra supply in a large bag over my shoulder. I would take the train into the city on Friday night and come back to school in New Jersey Sunday night with a stack of cash. Soon I recruited a bunch of my college friends to do it with me but none lasted more than two nights and quit. I could not figure out why they were not able to sell the garbage like I could. It was not just the inability to move the tacky merchandise that soured them on the job, it was the interactions of dealing with tourists who treated us much like the trash we were trying to sell them. Some of these guys were advanced business majors, who saw me coming home every weekend with a large wad of cash and figured that if I could do it, they, with all their business know-how, would be able to dominate the market. I would bring them in, teach them the pitch, give them their product, but what I could not give them was a steel jaw and thick skin. The first time they got grabbed by the arm and dragged out of a street festival for vending without a license, they were done. It was usually the cops that escorted you out of the area. Sometimes you would get a fine. No big deal, it got a little dicey when we would vend in Little Italy, on Mulberry Street, during the annual San Gennaro Festival. Once you experience being grabbed by the arms and dragged out by two Sicilian-speaking goombahs, and they take you to the main street via a smoke- and steam-filled alley, you realize that losing a night's pay was better than losing your thumbs. Most all those I recruited from my college would bail after one weekend.

In the winter, I worked for another vendor who would set up half a dozen stands in the East Village of NYC from October through December. We sold sweaters, gloves, and hats made from alpaca wool. I would stand behind a table on the sidewalk, on a piece of cardboard, from noon till midnight every day. The gig sucked, but for a future writer, it was a unique window of opportunity to observe and interact with all types of humanity. From homeless veterans to millionaire movie stars, I had the chance to meet them all. I had celebrities come by the stand, such as Jon Bon Jovi and Heather Locklear. Once, Robert Downey, Jr. picked up a sweater and told me it was for his then-girlfriend, Uma Thurman. He asked if I knew where he could get a unique pair of leather boots, and I walked him down the street to another vendor I knew who specialized in such footwear. I loved creating and trying out new pitches as people would walk past my stand. It was NYC, with all the attention-grabbing atmosphere of Greenwich Village, and I had to break through the tourist's trance and get them to notice my display.

The items we sold were not cheap, running upwards of sixty dollars per sweater, so the customers were not the same blinking-light-tchotchke-buying types I dealt with in the summer. Although we were still just a table on the street, the owner of the stand I worked for insisted the clothing items be arranged in a professional, appealing display. He would pay a homeless guy named Kenny to stand guard and ensure no one robbed the tables. The boss looked at me and said, "Don't be nervous, Kenny will look out for you." I hadn't been nervous, not until just then. I had met Kenny before. He had some vague military background that could not be clearly defined. He was talkative, which was okay. He was not a criminal, but he often talked about activities that were dancing right up to the edge. I recall one story where he was either shot or shot someone, but upon hearing the story twice, I still could not tell you which. The devil was in the details when you're working St. Marks Place, The Village. I tried to steer clear of details.

Upon graduating college, I worked pure sales. A little management, a little marketing, but I was a sales guy. Later, after finishing graduate school with an MBA in marketing and a minor in organizational development, I tried again and again to move into more traditional lines of corporate promotion and advertising, but I always ended up gravitating back to sales. It seemed I could not escape its grip. I did love representing the companies I worked for at trade shows and interacting with the crowds at the booths. Only by this point in my life, the booths I was manning were much more elaborate than a folding table on the street with a broken cardboard box for padding. The trade show booths now had two stories, conference rooms, video monitor displays, and usually a cappuccino bar. We would bring in attention grabbers such as hired models to hand out the corporate flyers (the talent had many names—"booth babes," "spokesmodels," "crowd gatherers," but in fact, they were the original influencers). It all boiled down to competing for the conference attendee's attention and ensnaring them with a tantalizing pitch about your product or service. While working a booth at a show, you learned simple-to-follow tricks that would help many an entrepreneur. Your body language mattered. Arms at your side, not crossed. Remain smiling and avoid resting bitch face, no matter how long you've been on the floor. Master the elevator pitch, and most importantly, get the attendee to breach the invisible barrier that delineated the space between your booth carpeting and the convention hall carpeting. If they were in the aisle, they were in no man's land. Once they stepped onto our overpriced, union-laid, rental carpet with foam padding, they were in our web.

I rarely would fatigue, even after hours of being peppered with questions by interested and interrogative prospects. I even enjoyed the give and take of competitors who would approach my booth and begin friendly conversations that I knew were a ruse for pumping me for information on products, contracts, and customers. I worked trade shows in the UK, Australia, United Arab Emirates, Brazil, and every region within the USA. I represented companies and products that ranged from consumer items to military technology. The people behind the booths were all outgoing, approachable, and eager to talk your ear off about whatever product was on display. The attendees understood that if they were at the conference, and especially on the trade show floor, they were open game. You did not need to feel any shyness or hesitation in approaching someone cold. It was not like a party, where you could spot someone you would like to engage with, but you had no idea if they were there to meet someone new or did not want to be approached.

Working in sales at trade shows is not dissimilar from speed dating. Everyone knew why everyone else was there, and that was to make a connection. I was now well-known in my industry. Everyone knew that if I was talking, I was pitching. And I knew if you were still standing there, you were at least willing to hear the pitch. If the pitch recipient was not interested, they could quickly and forthrightly tell me so with the knowledge that no offense would be taken. They knew I would be back in the future with a different pitch. Like Jurassic Park raptors, I would continue charging the electrified fence, always in a different spot, seeking the area that would allow me to break through.

I became what was then known as an "intrapreneur," someone who works on launching new projects, divisions, or technologies, but within the confines of a larger corporation.

When I established my own business, a sole-proprietor LLC, it was for the purpose of promoting my new book series. After decades of working only for others, this was my first stab at real entrepreneurship. I knew from the start I was not doing this to make a living. I knew I would probably not even make any money. That was never the purpose. I wanted people to read my books, my stories, and I wanted to become a recognized name within the fandom surrounding *The Walking Dead*.

I approached the literature and publishing world with the assumption that I would learn the craft of selling my books by listening to other authors sell theirs at their industry shows and conventions. After all, "sales is sales" and I had represented diverse industries and product lines. The successful sales approach, no matter the industry or the product or even the country, always seemed to follow a set formula, and I thought selling my own authored works would be no different. I would learn all I needed to know by observing other authors at conventions and listening to their sales pitch. Getting a salesman to talk was as easy as getting a zombie to bite—I could engage them in chatter and learn their marketing and promotional tricks. When I finally did meet the authors and illustrators, though, I found I was dead wrong.

It was comedic, even for me, the dissimilarity between myself—an aggressive, talkative, type-A extrovert—trying to interact with these talented, yet extremely introverted, sometimes-awkward authors and artists. Some would not even look up from whatever they were working on, writing, sketching, as I perused through their books and peppered them with questions.

Some struggled to quickly, concisely, explain their books' subject matter; the so-called "elevator pitch." Some seemed shell-shocked when I asked them pointed questions such as why they chose to become an author, how they got started, and where they planned on taking their writing career.

I recall asking one author how he promoted his books.

He hesitated and sheepishly replied, "Um…poorly."

I was not getting any wiser on what to do right, but I was getting schooled in what others were doing wrong. Luckily, that was also the year that Walker Stalker Con had their first event in New Jersey. While there have been horror-themed conventions around for many years, Walker Stalker was a convention just for fans of *The Walking Dead*. While I had grown up in NJ, I had relocated to northern Virginia years before. But New Jersey is not something you can simply just leave or even scrub off. It follows you. It embeds itself within you, within your DNA, like a virus. I had used New Jersey as the location for my Exit Zero book trilogy, and I always considered the state of NJ to be as essential to the storyline as any character in the book. When asked by people for the quick pitch on what my books were about, all I had to do is say "Zombies in New Jersey" and if I did not get a purchase, I at least would get a smile. When I saw a zombie-con was taking place in the Garden State, I drove north. I had hoped to spot some *TWD* celebrities and pick up some swag. I never got past the vending area. It was like my own Alexandria Safe Zone…I felt that I was among my own kind.

This is not a disparagement on the actors, whom I am sure are all talented and interesting people. But just being an actor on the show did not necessarily mean they were fans of the genre. If you were walking down the street and saw the actor who stared in the TV commercial for SnotBGone nasal spray, and you loved the SnotBGone product as it cured your lifelong case of the sniffles, would that actor be interested in hearing about your passion for that product? Would the actor be an expert in snoring relief, or wish to listen to your fanfiction ideas for a future commercial for SnotBGone? Of course not. He was an actor who filled a role and moved on to his next gig. Tomorrow he is shooting a commercial for irritable bowel syndrome and trust me, he does not want to hear your story ideas. The actors are cool, but I was not there to take a selfie. I was there to get ideas on how start and grow my fan-focused business.

I spent the entire day at my first Walker Stalker Con and never saw, or sought out, a single actor from the show. My time was consumed with just talking to the vendors and artists. To me, these were the most interesting people in the room. Some of the vendors are not much different than traditional retailers. They sell items such as mass-produced t-shirts, posters, and toys. I am sure many of these wholesale distributors are also fans of *TWD* and can carry their own when dealing with super-fans, talkers obsessed with walkers. But they, like the actors who appear in pop culture shows, are chameleons. They may be selling *TWD* merchandise today, but then will be selling entirely different-themed fandom t-shirts and toys at a sci-fi or sports-focused con the following week. We hear about Amazon and the Kardashians establishing "pop-up stores" like they invented something new. Wholesale con distributors have been doing it for decades.

If you want to talk to a hardcore fellow fan, someone who is as dedicated as you are to topic of the con you are attending, talk to an author, artist, or creator, who are generally grouped into the Artist Alley section. There you will find fellow travelers who have sacrificed their time and energy to craft tributes and mini-monuments to your shared fandom. You will read some of their stories and advice in this book.

My takeaway from these discussions was the understanding that as a fantrepreneur, the consumers of your creative talents are just like you, fans who want to talk about, create, and share their passion with other fans. That was the guidance I used towards becoming a fantrepreneur. I do not approach selling my books as if I am just selling books. I am sharing my own fandom of the genre that I hope fellow fans will take away as a souvenir from their visit in the zombie fandom universe. A parting gift as they leave the con, which served as a two-day *TWD* family reunion. A ticket to escape reality and enter the apocalyptic fun zone.

Before I get to the interviews of these fantrepreneurs, I will share with you my own unsolicited advice on what it will take to be successful in your first fan focused venture.

When you first rise, whisper rather than moan

We have all known that person who constantly talks about what they are going to do, but never does it. Quitting their job, writing a book, starting a diet, ending a relationship. Again, I am not criticizing them for not taking that next step from ideas and talk to planning and action. Creating momentum in life is hard, especially in a new direction. The annoyance factor comes from their constantly talking about how they *want* to do something which they never initiate, and then bitch and moan about what they have not accomplished. Don't be that person.

As you are contemplating your move towards fantrepreneurship, it is good to talk things out with people since sometimes, talking things through helps you better clarify and refine your concept and plans. Other times, you may hear your plan out loud for the first time and realize it sounded so much better when it was just an idea in your head. As soon as the concept hits the cold air of reality, it may begin to fall apart, like trying to remember a dream you were having immediately after waking up. There are also those who blab their great ideas to everyone who will listen, and then freak out when they see that idea come to fruition, only by someone else...one of the thousands of people they told it to.

When you are serious about taking your ideas forward, keep your conversations within a select group of friends and contacts. Tell them your plans and ask for their advice, but don't share this info with the world. Do not announce the space launch plans on Facebook and Twitter when you have not yet even built the rocket. There is a good chance the first or even fifth attempt at launch may fail. Wait till you have created something before you plan the release party. If you are not 100 percent certain on what artistic or business path you should follow, find as many people as you can who have already begun the journey and pump them for as much detail as they are willing to share without reporting you as a stalker.

Then, if you do choose to move forward, hold onto those contacts with a grip of death. I would say build your rolodex, but that is an outdated term. Instead I'll advise that you build your network, your following, and continue to update them with your progress. Networking is the life's blood of any business or artistic venture. Embrace all forms of technology to reach prospective clients and influencers. I am always surprised when I hear an artist say they don't have an account on (insert social media platform here). Yes, there are dozens of platforms out there and they all have as much bad associated with them as good, but they are all necessary.

Be prepared to utilize your connections like currency. The best way to get the word out to new prospects is to cross-promote with other vendors and artists in the space. Even if they are somewhat in a competitive space, if you have a positive relationship with the creator, it does not hurt to sometimes combine efforts. One day you compete for a client's dollar, another day you may team up to share the cost of appearing at a con by sharing a booth. There may be times when you are going to work on a new project, and you can inform your fans that while you won't be seen at upcoming cons, you suggest they visit another artist that you respect. Hopefully that artist will return the favor. The term is compet-a-mates (competitors/teammates), another word-mashup meaning your competitor is not your enemy, more like a frenemy. Again, with the word mash.

When I meet new fantrepreneurs, I often will offer them a social media shout-out to my own contact list if, in exchange, they will offer a promotion of my books to theirs. This seems like a crass exploitation of relationships, because that is exactly what it is. If you do not feel confident enough in your product to promote it to your friends, you should not be promoting it to strangers.

Keep looking at the flowers

Creating, writing, and starting a new business will be a lonely and isolating undertaking.

Madness brought about by isolation is the second leading cause of death in the zombie apocalypse genre. In the film *The Night Eats the World*, it is not the zombies that are the biggest threat to the protagonist, but his crippling solitude.

But solitude is necessary, and when you do set aside time to think, work and create, you need to focus only on the task at hand—nothing else. Life will go on outside your work space. You just won't be part of it, which can be difficult for some. There are a thousand things to distract you: social media should be used only if you are promoting your business. Otherwise, don't get lured in, trust me, nothing on there is as important as your new venture.

Learn to separate your business fandom from your family fandom. Fandom is a wonderful thing to share with your spouse and kids, but if you are becoming a fantrepreneur, the lines can blur so you need to set clear boundaries. This can be especially tricky when you are exhibiting and selling your product or service at a con. I have met creators whose families will accompany them to the con and have a pre-organized plan for making that con appearance a success. The family all show up wearing matching promotional t-shirts. The wife, husband, mother, father, kids are all walking around the con to hand out flyers about the business and are bringing attendees and prospective customers over to the booth. If the artist or author needs a break, they are there to sit in and man the booth with attentiveness. These families serve as a support structure and greatly enhance the potential for success of the business.

Then I have seen vendors bring family members who obviously do not want to be there. They are bored and irritated. At best, they are a distraction to the vendor, and at worst, an annoyance and sale killer. I know that seems harsh, but it's true. When you have a booth at a con, and in sales and promotion mode, you need to focus 100 percent of that time on growing your business. Your spouse and kids may not understand why you are going to a fun and exciting comic- or horror-focused convention for the entire weekend and not bringing them. People go to work at Disneyland every day, but they don't bring their kids along. It may be the Happiest Place on Earth, but that happiness is for the guests. Everyone else is there to work and that is what you're doing at the con, working.

Besides, if you think this business venture will also be a way to have fun, family-together time, think again. First, your family will grow bored at the con—if not within a couple hours, then by the second day. If they are not bored, they will be spending all the profits you make while trying to kick off your new business. If you want to spend time at a con with your family, go as a guest, not as a vendor.

During the start-up phase of your new fantrepreneurship, understand that even when you are home with your family, you will be lucky to give them 50 percent of your time and attention, and that is being generous. You may be physically there, but you won't be present. If your family is not on board, think twice if this is the time to start a fan-based venture. For entrepreneurs, when you are running your business, you are thinking about your business. When you are with your family, you are thinking about your business. If you're not, you probably won't be in business for long.

Don't worry, your friends and family will still be there for you. It's all about balance. For me, I find working at night is the most productive. From 10:00 p.m. till 1:00 a.m. is the peak performance period for me. Late enough that family is not in need of my attention, but early enough to get in enough sleep to function the next day. When I am in create mode, my family knows they won't see me in the late-night hours.

If you are an extrovert like me, who derives your energy from interaction with other people, it is difficult to close yourself off. Once you set that time to create, and settle down alone to do so, you will remember every single item on your "To Do" list. You will hear conversations in your house that you are not part of. You will hear music from the best party of the year in the neighboring dorm. You will hear laughter from your roommates. You need to find your inner Adderall and focus on the flowers.

If you are an introvert, the solitude will not be as difficult to deal with. You probably would not have been invited to the party down the hall anyway and the roommate laughter is probably at your expense. That is fine, as most introverts have already mastered the art of self-quarantine. But don't get cocky, introverts, your challenges will come later when it is time to promote.

Carving out an hour or two a day, or even a week, to just focus on creating, sounds like it could be a challenge…but I'm sure you do it already without realizing. Investing an hour of your time every week just to watch *TWD* is a calculated risk. There are always trade-offs and opportunity costs. There are many more important things you could have been focused on during that one hour of *TWD* time. Organizing your finances, doing the laundry, reporting blood curdling screams from your neighbor's house.

But you have made the decision to block it all out and watch your favorite show. You have already mastered the art of focus.

Besides, the screams eventually ceased; after all, every new neighbor is an opportunity for a new friend. Ask any serial killer.

My Network Belongs to Negan

For any fan of *TWD*, their relationship to the character of Negan is complex. He is vicious, ruthless and kills off some of the fan favorite characters. Yet he can be also charming and in his own way, quite successful in running his own start-up enterprise of The Saviors. Negan advises his followers that, "people are resources and should not be wasted." This is good advice from a bad man.

Beginning from the very launch of your venture, you will need to grow and nurture your resources. As your artistic efforts or business plans begins to take shape, those resources are needed to provide you critical feedback. Never close yourself off to the voices providing negative feedback. While you do not need to follow all advice or take all criticisms and artistic critiques to heart, you still need to listen.

You also need to have thick skin. Thicker than any zombie could bite through. Harsh negative criticism of something you have labored over can feel like rotted teeth ripping flesh from bone. Embrace the hate. Revel in rejection. Do *not* argue with people who give negative opinions on your work, especially on social media. Accept all inputs and use them to better navigate a path forward.

For instance, if no one likes your product, not even the sub-sub-sub subsets of fandom for whom you're creating, then you must make some hard choices. If you are fine with creating something that only you, and maybe a single likeminded weirdo, would find pleasing, then go forth and continue creating as much unappreciated art as the world can stomach. I have seen horror-themed fantrepreneurs who have created items that even I, a zombie fan, find creepy and off-putting. But who the hell cares what I think? They obviously have a customer base to sustain their business, and for that, they have my undying respect.

Don't feel like a failure if you do not find a mass market that shares your aesthetic. If you find a single fan who is willing to pay you for your creative work, you are a success at *you* being *you*.

But if your goal is the pursuit of the hearts and wallets of a larger audience, then you will need to adapt your vision and incorporate other, more mass-appeal elements into your final product.

The result may not be 100 percent your own, but don't worry, you will still love the baby, even if you know in your heart, it is as much Shane's as it is yours.

Avoid becoming an Apoca-Cliché

When you watch a typical zombie/post-apocalyptic story, there are repeated clichés where characters make foolish decisions or put themselves into harm's way due to needless distraction, poor delegation of tasks, or the inability to recognize what everyone else around them has already acknowledged.

Yet I have seen these clichéd scenes appear again and again in movies and TV. This is not due to laziness of the writer. These often-repeated storylines are added to films as they are real-world situations that the writers and directors have experienced, and it bled into their works. I call them Apoca-Clichés.

In both the film *World War Z* and apocalyptic series *The Rain*, the setups for the opening sequence are nearly identical. The apocalypse begins. The family tries to escape by car with the father driving, mother in the passenger seat, and two annoying kids in the back seat. Kids won't buckle up, mom is incapable of getting them to comply, so dad, who is currently navigating the vehicle at 90 mph through a serpentine obstacle course of wrecked cars and flying bodies, must turn around, taking his eyes off the road, to buckle in the kids. At that moment in time, when the father had one important task to complete, he was distracted trying to do something the other three people in the car should have handled themselves. In both cases, his action leads to a wrecked car and a family jog through madness and mayhem. Really?

As a fantrepreneur, learn to both delegate non-essential tasks and accept help from others. If you are an artist, and your business is going gangbusters, but you realize that 75 percent of your time is spent managing your social media promotion, answering email inquiries, and handling the day-to-day business activities like booking con appearances, contacting galleries, and collecting money, then you are not investing your time appropriately. Understand well in advance before you start a new venture that for it to succeed, you will require the full, unwavering support of friends and family. That support also extends to leaving you alone and giving you your personal space when necessary. When you begin a new venture, especially if this is the first time your family has experienced you working from home, they need to buy into the fact that while they *see* you at home, you are *not there*. You are working. You can foster this understanding by ensuring they see you are indeed working, and not just surfing the web claiming research. Remember, they can always go back and track your browser history. Make sure you set those boundaries.

If you have people around you who are there to help, accept their help. If you don't have any friends or family willing to provide support, be prepared to pay strangers for that support.

Also, I would recommend the Dale Carnegie book *How to Win Friends and Influence People*.

Only you can create your art. The quality of your product or service is what will make your business successful. Let friends, family or hired staff handle the mundane. You create what only you can create. Let everyone else attend to everything else.

This is especially true when you are exhibiting and selling your works at a con. During show hours, you must be 100 percent present. Make eye contact with attendees as they walk past your booth. Don't leer, mind you, but find that happy medium where you can lock eyes with attendees in a way that displays warm receptiveness and not lonely desperation for human contact.

A con booth is a substantial investment, and exhibitor hours are limited. Don't spend that time looking at your phone, writing your next book, or sketching your next masterpiece. Understand that, besides the cost of the booth space, there are opportunity costs. The time at a show is time spent selling your past works, not creating new ones. Take this into consideration before booking an event. If you are crushing on three deadlines to deliver new content for a customer, don't book a show. If you are booked at an annual show which you registered for months in advance, schedule your deliverables to be completed prior, so you are not frantically trying to finish while manning your booth when you are supposed to be selling.

The dead may walk the earth for eternity. The entrepreneur needs to practice good time management.

Piss people off

What is ironic is when you are at the initial stages of creating, it will be very difficult to find someone willing to provide you critical feedback and allow you to use them as a sounding board for ideas. Whether you're writing a book, crafting a business plan, recording a podcast, or sketching your first illustration, no one will want to read, view, listen, or critique your work. But once it is finished and you are officially established as a business, promoting and selling your wares on the market, everyone you know will expect a freebie.

Learn to say no. Free samples of your work are for true influencers. Those reviewers or personalities who have amassed a large audience of the chosen fanbase you are targeting. Preferably, those influencers who are inclined to give you a positive public endorsement. Everyone else is a potential paying customer. If you do not feel confident enough in your product to ask your friends and family to pay for it, then you are not ready to officially launch your entrepreneurial venture.

This is just my two cents—it's ultimately your call. If providing your creations to anyone who asks free of charge makes your heart swell with joy and the warm humanity of giving, go for it. Damn hippie.

Yeah, I am talking about you, Aunt Joan, who reminds me every time I see you that I should *give* you a copy of my book. No, Aunt Joan, you have an Amazon account. Besides, you are not my target demographic. You are not a social media influencer. You are not even my favorite aunt.

Cold, yes. The transition from hobbyist to entrepreneur can be as gut-wrenching as the transition from human to zombie. In both, there is a good chance of insomnia, abandonment, and frequent vomiting. To paraphrase Tallahassee in *Zombieland*, "Time to nut up or shut up."

Don't piss people off

The value of pop culture, as with any art form, is subjective and always at the whims of a fickle public. It is a constantly shifting consumer market. A TV show, book, movie, or celebrity that displayed absolute dominance of their respective field one year could be the butt of jokes and scorn the following year. The fantrepreneur is generally tethering their wagon to a product of someone else's creative talents. If they sink like the Titanic, you are going down with the ship. It is not unfair to say that you are swimming in that creator's wake. If that creator decides to throw a bucket of rancid chum over the side of the boat, you're going to be the most vulnerable to the social media sharks that come for the feeding frenzy. When you have built a business around a specific pop-culture icon, your entire venture could be wiped out at the speed it takes to send a late-night, Ambien-fueled tweet.

All fandom communities have standards, which are managed through both fan community enforcement and self-moderation. With any type of identity-based gathering and identity-based consumerism, there will be outliers. Even in groups that relish being considered outside the norm, there will be the fringe element. Fandom "standards of conduct" generally do not need to be posted and are usually self-policed by fellow fandom. Good-natured rivalry within fandoms can lead to lively, hours-long debates about the utterly meaningless, such as the earlier mentioned differentiation between fast and slow-moving zombies. On the contrary, there are those that not only love their chosen fandom, but express and formulate animosity towards opposing tracks of fandom—such as *The Walking Dead* vs. *Z-Nation* vs. *iZombie*.

As the sole brand ambassador of your business venture, an "us versus them" argument could be a tightrope you may be forced to walk. It is best to remain neutral from a public persona about such hot topics. Once you become an entrepreneur, your personal social media postings are indistinguishable from your professional postings. Avoid any type of comments, alignments, or endorsements that could be turn-offs for potential buyers and business partners. Keep all tweets, postings, responses, and retweets about your product and your brand. You are not investing your time and money into a business to fight with strangers online over topics in which you are not involved. Unless, of course, your entrepreneurial venture has a business plan that involves somehow monetizing the activity of fighting with strangers online. I am sure there are professional trolls and flamethrowers, but if that is your field, I would not consider you really to be a fantrepreneur.

You may think this sounds elementary, like something being told to a fifth-grader about "what you put online will be there forever," but I have seen the most professional, self-disciplined and business-minded people lose their freaking minds on Twitter and Facebook. Posting long diatribes or getting into tweet wars over topics of which they know little, events where they were not present, or people they will never meet. All they accomplished was to turn off customers and influencers, who either have an opposing view, or just do not want to be associated with someone getting into public social media spats.

There is an adage in sales along the lines of: *Once you have made the sale, shut up. Anything more you say can delay or even kill the deal.* We used to call it diarrhea of the mouth, a disgusting visual, but an apt metaphor for someone who could not stop talking. In the past, a business owner who would not stop until their foot was in their mouth caused damage that was contained to those who were in the room at the time. Now, we have diarrhea of the digital footprint. If you are really angry about something, scream into your pillow until you fall asleep. Trust me, when you wake up, you will feel better and you won't find yourself unfriended.

All pop culture can come with its own toxic baggage. Standing or kneeling in sports, boycotts by musicians, controversial topics addressed in comic books, political pronouncements by actors tightly associated with your fandom. Do not feel that you can weigh in on any topic, I repeat, *any topic*, without understanding that there is the potential of blowback. Once more, think long and hard before posting something that could alienate current or future customers, partners and fans. Your posts have the possibility of being discovered a decade later, when perhaps you have different priorities in life. Yesterday's immediate gratification of tweeting your opinion to that millionaire singer who just said something stupid and you need to set her straight, because "Dammit, you must get it off your chest!" may lead you to losing a financially lucrative opportunity tomorrow.

While you want your artwork and literature and business plans to be exciting, unique and attention-grabbing, you also want your public position on hot-button issues to be neutral or at least vague. We good? Enough said? Now go delete all those drunken, "it was oh so funny and clever at the time," or angry, self-important tweets…*now*!

The real world can be just as ugly and awkward as the web. Despite your best efforts, sometimes you will also be thrust into uncomfortable, real-world situations that don't involve your laptop or phone. Yes, that ugly, coffee-fueled, non-cyber realm called reality. You may be at a con, or a business meeting, or just meeting fans, and someone will ask you your opinion on a topic that you do *not* want to address. You know that in whatever direction you take your next step, it will be into a steaming pile of shit. An "are you Team Rick or Team Negan?" type of demand for allegiance.

It happened to me, I was unprepared, and my response was idiotic. I was working for a firm as an intrapreneur and I received a request to go to the Middle East to make a presentation to that country's military. My company brought in a "Middle East expert" to provide some guidance on the region. Knowing that my last name could be controversial for some,

I asked him outright what I should do if they asked me if I was Jewish. The expert advised me that it was a question which would never be asked. I pressed for advice on how to respond, just in case. He assured me that I would never, under any circumstance, be asked that question within any professional setting.

After a fourteen-hour flight, and two extra days of sitting in my hotel room due to the meeting being inexplicably delayed (yes, that is a cliché that is absolutely true), I was finally brought in to make my presentation. As I booted up my laptop, my interpreter handed out my cards and presentation packet to the attendees. The most senior officer in the room picked up my card, leaned back in his chair as he examined it, then read my name aloud asking: "Neil Cohen....This is a Jewish name, correct?"

I stammered for a moment, totally unprepared. Then the words left my lips: "Well, I am not quite sure of the lineage of the name. I believe it may be Scottish." I don't know where that came from and I mentally slapped my forehead with my palm. As if my grandparents arrived on Ellis Island after fleeing the castles of Edinburgh and decided to drop the O' from our last name of "O'Cohen" to make it sound less ethnic. Having followed only the advice of the "expert" and not my own gut instinct, I had not prepared any canned responses.

Another awkward example was at a con where a blogger wanted to interview me. This does happen a lot at cons and you can usually tell the more professional bloggers and podcasters based upon the quality of their equipment or if they are in a group with a video, sound, and/or lighting person accompanying the interviewer. Then there are those that pull out their phone to film or record you. Either way, be cautious. This interview was one of those solo, "I am filming you with my phone" guys and he came by my booth and asked twice before

I relented to be interviewed. The questioning was benign and covered about five minutes of Q&A about my books and the zombie genre. He then followed up with a question about my favorite topic of nonfiction, and I replied that I was reading a civil war biography. He had turned the camera off at this point but proceeded to provide me his conspiracy theories about the civil war that were well outside anything you would ever hear on The History Channel. I politely moved him along but decided from that point forward, I needed to request a website URL and view the requestor's blog or podcast site *before* accepting any future interview requests.

I always try to anticipate any possible apocalyptic Q&A scenario that my mind can conjure up, so as to pre-plan diplomatic responses. It used to be simple—avoid religion and politics and you would be okay. Those are days gone by. In person or online, keep topics focused on your business and the products or services you provide. What do you do if you want to have lively conversations and friendly debates about the pressing matters of the day? Hey, don't look at me, I have no advice for you. And If I did, I would keep it to myself so as not to piss anyone off.

Failure is always an option

Failure, like salt, is good for you in moderation. I am intimately familiar with failure. I have failed at many things: business deals, relationships, drug tests. With failure comes knowledge, and that knowledge can be passed onto others, in the hopes that their failures may be even more spectacular, making yours look less painful in hindsight.

People love to hear about failures. *Schadenfreude*, or the pleasure in others' misfortune, is what makes us human. You can't learn anything from someone who has had the greatest luck in the world, nor can you learn from someone who has spent their life without taking any risks.

One of the biggest lessons from failure is recognizing when you have failed, and then making the difficult decisions. Sometimes you can put your heart and soul into a project, but you were missing one ingredient. For instance, let's say talent. It is not that you have no talent, it's just that you don't have any talent in that one field. There are no participation trophies in entrepreneurship. You need to be very self-aware of your own limitations. I know this sounds like the worst pep talk in locker room history, but disappointment is cheap, launching a bound-to-fail venture is not.

For example, I wanted to be an actor since the age of seven. My father was in plays and my aunt was a singer in New York. I thought I had it in the genes. I took acting lessons, read all the books, appeared in all the high school plays, even starred in a few. I spent a fortune on acting coaches, headshots, demo reels, and traveling to auditions. But the truth was, I was awful. I stunk up the stage, but I wanted it so bad that I was nose-blind and did not catch a whiff. Wasted time, wasted money, and worse of all, wasted opportunities where I could have been approaching the market from a different angle. I ignored my natural talents of sales and could have entered the show business world representing actors or productions. But I held on to a business model for too long. In the venture capital world, they call these start-ups "zombie companies." The product has failed, the good people have left, yet the CEO and a couple core people hang on, still desperate to save the company, not acknowledging it is already dead.

A common theme in *TWD* is how a character will react when they realize a companion has been bitten. There are those that immediately accept the truth and, without hesitation, do what they need to do and shoot their friend or family member in the head to avoid future suffering. They embrace the reality that once a major bite has occurred, the situation is hopeless and any attempts to save that person will just prolong the suffering of the infected and increase the risk of further loss to those around them. They move quickly and efficiently to end the situation, shed a tear, and move on.

Then there are those that just cannot accept the reality of the situation. They put their bitten loved ones in a barn, or in the cellar, tie them up, or believe that they can mitigate the loss by hacking off the arms and pulling out the teeth. They end up further destroying that which they once embraced, mutilating what they once loved, in a futile attempt to sustain it for a while longer. This always leads to disaster, both on the show and in real-life entrepreneurship. Really, really, *really* wishing for something won't make it so. Sorry Oprah.

You need to approach your new venture in the vein of the former, not the latter. If your concept is not working, be prepared to cut your losses and just walk away. You should have a set dollar amount that you and your family have decided to invest. If you have breached that threshold and you see no signs of life in your venture, pull that trigger and bury the corpse deep.

Don't worry, there is always one more failure waiting just down the road. Just like navigating a zombie-strewn landscape, you know the failures are there waiting for you. Some are very visible, shambling down the center of the road, and some are hidden, like a legless torso beneath a car snapping at your ankles. If you are always anticipating the worst and do not take unnecessary risks, you will survive the journey.

In other words, keep your focus, plan your moves, listen to advice (even if you choose not to follow it all), and accept critical feedback from those you respect. Don't take failure personally, maintain self-awareness and continue to believe strongly in the value of what you are bringing to the fanbase.

Question before you Con

Always continue to ask questions, both of others and yourself, at every step of your business venture, and never stop.

Rick Grimes would pose three questions to strangers he encountered, before considering them for the Alexandria community:

1. "How many walkers have you killed?"

2. "How many people have you killed?"

3. "Why?"

My questions to anyone who is considering fantrepreneurship:

1. "How many times have you tried?"

2. "How many times have you failed?"

3. "Why?"

The answers I would give to Rick Grimes's three questions are identical to the answers I would give to my own three questions:

1. Too many to count.

2. Too few to matter.

3. Why not?

I have spoken much about how important cons are to the fantrepreneur, especially when first launching your venture, and while I feel they are pivotal to success, they are also one of the largest expenses you will face—so don't go unprepared.

What are your objectives for the con? Your booth display should clearly and intuitively convey that you are there to sell your product or raise awareness of your charity or promote a service which attendees can take advantage of at a future date—such as a tour of filming locations or a themed escape room. If attendees stare curiously at your booth, your display, or your banner, and still must ask what it is that you do, you blew it.

What do you want to walk away with at the end of the con? Whether it is a fistful of cash and credit card orders, or a couple hundred email addresses for future follow-up, decide before you go what constitutes a success. Please be aware that it won't happen at your first con. You should plan on attending the same con three or four times before people begin to really take notice of you and your exhibit. This is a journey.

Reach out to the con organizer before you exhibit to learn about the types of people who attend and if your product or service will resonate with them. Sometimes it is not that obvious to identify what is and is not a good marketing opportunity. I spoke to one fantrepreneur who was launching a sci-fi-themed conference. He launched his new venture at an anime-focused con. On the surface, these two tracks of fandom seem like a natural fit together. Futuristic settings, space aliens, and other worlds are commonplace in anime, yet he found interest in his new conference to be non-existent. I do not have an answer for you as to exactly why, but upon speaking to other sci-fi vendors, they told me they had the same experience.

But the most important question is one you should ask yourself. Do you know why you want to become a fantrepreneur? If so, does your perception mesh with reality?

Do you want to find love? Well, if you are single, I can tell you the rumors are true. Once you officially launch your business, publish your first book, or create your first piece of art, you won't have to worry about waking up alone ever again.

Every night will become a threesome. Every morning, you will open your bleary eyes, roll your head on your barely-used pillow, and view the yellow notepad and pen lying next to you. The pad will be filled with all the scribbled thoughts that kept you awake the night before. All the things you forgot to do yesterday, all the things you must complete today, all the ideas that seemed brilliant at three in the morning, and tasks you will need to complete on a nonexistent day off, like going to Costco and buying more yellow notepads because you ran out.

If you are married, well then congratulations; it appears con nerds can find love. Hey, I just invented another word mash-up: ConNerds. If you are married and you are still trying to find love, well, there are also many books out there on that topics as well—but this is not one of them. If you are married, in love, and want to start your fantrepreneurship, then make sure your spouse is on board, as they will deal with the ups and downs of starting and running this new venture as much as you will. You will need their unwavering support. When your spouse walks into your home office and says, "Since you are home today, could you...," do not finish their sentence with, "Can I focus on my work and nothing else, completely blocking out all other distractions including what you are about to ask me to do? Yes, yes, I can do that." Trust me, this is not conducive to a happy home/work life balance. You will end up sleeping with nothing but the yellow note pad again.

As for your kids, they can be 'volun-told' to be on board. Another word mash-up of volunteer and told. Hopefully, they will find the experience of supporting your pop culture-themed venture as enjoyable as you will spending time with your kids. That has been one of the most unexpected benefits of my own experience. My kids, for the first time, are eager to tell their friends about their dad's zombie business.

Do you want to get rich? If you are thinking that becoming a fantrepreneur will allow you to quit your day job, kill that idea right now. Kill it with fire and then bury the ashes. The fantrepreneurial venture should be about a temporary escape from reality. If you hate your job, find a new job, or pursue the traditional entrepreneurial route and form a business that will ensure you an income. Fantrepreneurship should be approached for the riches you will gain in new experiences, meeting new people, and the joy it provides. You cannot pay your mortgage with the residuals of personal fulfillment.

Do you want to get revenge? Go rent a Liam Neeson movie. Any one, they are all the same.

Do you want to have fun, do good deeds, create new things and meet new people? Then continue forward and launch your fantrepreneurship. You are the perfect candidate for the job. Hire yourself.

CHAPTER THREE

THE DAWN OF THE FANTREPRENEUR

"If you connect your fandom well with other fields, you can have a real impact."

—*FROM AN INTERVIEW WITH NICOLLE LAMERICHS,*
Author, Blogger, Researcher

I reached out to Nicolle Lamerichs, pop culture researcher, author of the book *Productive Fandom* and originator of the term "fantrepreneur." While she was traveling extensively in Europe, she made time to be interviewed about how she came to this field of study.

I found you when researching the term "fantrepreneur." Do you know if you are the first person to use that term within a professional publication?

Yes, I presented my research at a conference in 2018 and all my work is posted on my blog. I'm currently working on another research article that further dissects the term, which should be out by 2020. I am glad that the topic and term resonates! I use it to describe those fans who engage in business and entrepreneurial activities. I have also used the term "fan-centric economy" a lot, for the deep platform economy that we are in, which caters to the avid fans and users. A fan-centric economy is one that increasingly profits from fans, introducing premium models and tiers for website access and con tickets (VIP or Gold tickets as opposed to standard entry passes). With fan-driven platforms like Kickstarter and Legion M, we are looking at a world in which fans have become investors as well.

You yourself are the author of the book Productive Fandom, *how did "fandom studies" become of interest?*

When I read early fan and fandom studies by Matt Hills, Henry Jenkins, and Nancy Baym, I became interested in the field and wanted to explore it further. I received a grant for the study of cultural dynamics, and from that I was able to do a substantial research project on it, which laid the groundwork for *Productive Fandom* and many of my other articles.

Do you feel this is an area of research that you can build a career upon?

Whether you can build a career on it, I think you can, and I think to some extent I have. You can check out my personal website to see the cool projects that I'm involved in. Some of these are broader projects, such as a cosplay exhibition which I co-curated in a showroom in Rotterdam. When it's purely about academic research, I think studying fans truly is worthwhile. Many companies invest in this, though sometimes under different terms such as "brand ambassadors" or "influencers." In academia and universities, it's tricky. I tend to frame fandom as an example of a topic that I put into a broader context, such as Studies of the Modern Consumption Society. These studies can be useful in both business and academic fields. Only presenting yourself as a Fandom Scholar would do both you and the field an injustice. I think if you connect your fandom-focused business well with other fields, such as marketing, advertising, business strategy research, and public relations, you can have a real impact.

What do you feel are the differences between fandom in the USA as compared to fandom in the UK, Netherlands, and other regions you have researched around the world?

There are many, many differences. I highlighted these in an article I wrote called "The Cultural Dynamic of Doujinshi and Cosplay." In Japan, for instance, fandom is a very clear part of the urban landscape. While there is still some stigma around some particular fandoms (e.g., manga fandom), fandom has become a major focus of shopping districts. Japan has a big gift and consumption culture, with many local mascots and characters. Japanese society is very structured and hierarchical. So, fandom reflects a different role in society in Japan than it does in America, because the societies are so different.

Fandom in The Netherlands is quite small. Fans organized their own conventions just for each other and would only draw three hundred to five hundred visitors. These small events still exist, but now, large, professionally run conventions are popping up. Nothing compared to the UK, but in terms of fan practices, the countries heavily overlap.

Have you identified any specific attributes that make a successful fantrepreneur?

Not yet, but that's certainly something I want to investigate more. It's always difficult to say what makes one fandom-based businesses go viral and others not. Some tentative thoughts based on what I have seen so far:

- A solid business model matters, as it always does in all entrepreneurship. If you have a unique selling point, other fans will buy from you. If you are the only one recreating the "Ocarina of Zelda," people know where to find you. If you have conceived of a shirt design or piece of jewelry that no one else has recreated, it helps.

- Proper valuation means asking the right price for your goods and service and not overcharging for fan-made merchandise.

- Attracting influencers. To do so, you must keep uploading new content, keep providing new things to see, and really be fan-worthy.

- Word of mouth: If you create beautiful costumes or commissions, word can spread quite quickly. I think fan status goes hand in hand with success. As Kevin Kelly of *Wired* Magazine writes, you only need one thousand true fans to achieve success.

What advice would you give someone who is considering this path, and is unsure if they are ready to make the investment of time and money necessary to launch a fan-based business?

A fan business is not different from any other type of business. Do your research and invest enough time investigating if there is a market. If you are a novice, find a business model template form and have it walk you through building a plan. [That] is always one of the best tools to use and fill in. If it's just a few buttons or pieces of fan art that you are selling, don't overthink it. Invest that time in your craft. But for bigger projects, like starting a shop or a more complicated business, I would truly think and plan out your concept fully. For instance, conduct surveys among potential customers, or start by showcasing your creative works at a table at a small fan convention to see how they respond. The good thing with fans is, you can approach them easily online and in person.

Showcasing your product prototypes and first creations online is a good and low-cost way to see how people respond. Start on eBay or a website with an "order" button to see if people respond. If it's a larger-level project, get investors on board. I hosted some small cons without any sponsorship, but I really wouldn't recommend that. While we managed to break even, I think if we had taken such projects more seriously, it would have been less stressful for us and less risky [than] investing from my own pocket.

Have you observed horror genre, or more specifically, zombie genre type fandom-focused business while conducting your research?

I have observed some aspects of it, particularly the cross-over between the zombie genre in television, and how it then revived in board games (e.g., Dead of Winter) and digital games (e.g., Last of Us). It's truly in a revival, and older gothic tropes are there. Zombies, and any type of monster really, often reflect societal fear. It's interesting to compare older zombie films, which echoed a fear about consumer culture and mass media, with current zombies, that are much more post-9/11. The current trend, which *Twilight* also reflects, of zombies and monsters learning to really care about human characters (e.g., *Warm Bodies*) also fascinates me. I think *True Blood* was also a key show in this respect. By normalizing vampires through production of artificial blood, they became more human and had to interact with humans in a different way. This also allowed the show to approach *otherness* in a different way, not through themes of fear, but by shedding light on diversity and discrimination. The show ends extremely hopeful.

CHAPTER FOUR

WRITING THE DEAD

Jay Bonansinga, Author, Director, and Co-writer of *The Walking Dead* book series

"The best things in your life, in your career, come from being a fan of others."

- ✔ *2011 The Walking Dead: Rise of the Governor* (with Robert Kirkman)

- ✔ *2012 The Walking Dead: The Road to Woodbury* (with Robert Kirkman)

- ✔ *2012 Just Another Day at the Office: A Walking Dead Short* (with Robert Kirkman)

- ✔ *2013 The Walking Dead: The Fall of the Governor* (with Robert Kirkman)

- ✔ *2014 Robert Kirkman's The Walking Dead: Descent*

- ✔ *2015 Robert Kirkman's The Walking Dead: Invasion*

- ✔ *2016 Robert Kirkman's The Walking Dead: Search and Destroy*

- ✔ *2016 Self Storage*

- ✔ *2017 Robert Kirkman's The Walking Dead: Return to Woodbury*

As I stated earlier, I blame my obsession with zombies on being exposed to them when I was too young. Jay Bonansinga was also traumatized as a young child, but by a character much more animated than the zombies. His childhood fear was born from a night at the drive-in with his grandparents to see *101 Dalmatians*. It was through confronting this childhood trauma caused by the monochromatic Cruella Deville that he chose to pursue a career in both writing and scaring others. Jay taught himself how to become a writer by—literally—copying novels of great writers such as Hemingway and Faulkner. He re-typed their entire novels so that he could experience how authors frame their content.

In my discussion with Jay, I asked how he become the author chosen by Robert Kirkman to craft both origin stories of the well-known characters from *The Walking Dead* comic and TV series, as well as create entirely new storylines not previously covered by television or comics.

He recounted his own fandom for the genre and told the story of the original *TWD* comic series' origin. Robert Kirkman had just finished watching the George Romero film *Dawn of the Dead* and, at the end of the movie asked, "And then what...?" Kirkman's answer to that question was the creation of *The Walking Dead* graphic novel series, which was followed by the AMC TV series, which was followed by Jay's *The Walking Dead* book series.

Jay was not a zombie neophyte when he landed the job to write the Governor series. His first book, *The Black Mariah*, was purchased 1992 by New Line Cinema. It was every writer's dream. A film was to be made based on his book. He was asked to be a co-writer of the screenplay, and to make things more surreal, the director who he would work with was none other than a legend within the zombie genre, the horror icon George Romero, who invited Jay to stay with him at his home to create the script. I asked Jay why I had never heard of the movie and the story Jay recounted of what followed is an important lesson in resilience for any entrepreneur.

Jay's book was about a truck driver who was placed under a perpetual motion curse, which would not allow him to slow or stop his vehicle without bursting into flames. Jay had been working with George, writing the script, for several weeks when one day the phone rang. George answered, and Jay could ascertain from the conversation that the caller was someone from New Line film production. "No, I had not heard of that movie," George responded into the receiver in response to the caller's question. He turned around to face Jay and asked, "Have you heard of a film that is in final production called *Speed* with some guy named Keanu Something?"

A great story as well as a great life lesson. Setbacks, and the ability to overcome them, is essential for any fantrepreneur. The industry is fickle and fluid. But Jay told me that he is first and foremost a writer, which is all he ever wanted to be, other than being a fan of course.

He faced this and future challenges by understanding that there are certain axioms in the arts that will never change...the constants, such as how you tell a story, and how the fan base consumes that story.

"It's biological. We live, we die, and in between we experience, hear, and tell stories. That is why stories are told and will always be a strong commodity for any fantrepreneur who wants to pursue the tract of writing, filmmaking, or sequential illustrations." His advice is to never push back on input people give you. "Absorb it, respect it, even if you don't incorporate it. Ultimately it will be your decision as to what your product will be. Great ideas come from the thin line between brilliance and absurdity," Jay told me in one of our discussions.

When Jay is asked to attend a con by a show organizer to promote his books, he never turns them down. But he understands that when he is at a con, it is time away from his writing. He stresses to me the importance of engineering your professional and promotional life. "There is a need to monetize your time and level of efforts, as there is always the balance of accepting opportunity costs versus immediate revenue goals. When you are behind the table at a con, or speaking at a panel session, or promoting yourself in some way online or in some other medium, you are focusing your time on selling your prior works. When you are alone in your studio or office, you won't recognize immediate return, as that is an investment of time creating future works. If you spend all your time creating, you will quickly deplete all your revenues and resources. Yet if you rest on your laurels and spend all your time and focus promoting your existing products, you will either run out of fans or slip into irrelevancy." Jay approaches his business with the Francis Ford Coppola theory. The director of *Apocalypse Now* and *The Godfather* had a sign on his office door that read: Fast, Cheap, Good. Choose two.

Although primarily an author, Jay has scaled his business to include corporate speaking gigs, providing his philosophy on fostering creativity within the corporate environment. Spoiler alert, creativity does not just appear while sitting in a cubicle between 9:00 a.m. and 5:00 p.m. Jay's only warning to future entrepreneurs is that becoming a fantrepreneur will fundamentally change the dynamic between you and the object of your fandom. He summarizes this guidance this way: "But if there is love there, your efforts may cause you to suffer—to miss out on some other aspects of life—but will also produce great joy. As long as you approach your business based on your love and fandom, it will be worth it."

CHAPTER FIVE

TALKING THE DEAD

"I focus on strong production values, interesting guests and fun that is infectious for the audience."
—JASON CABASSI, *Host of* The Walking Dead 'Cast,
founder of Podcastica, and Panel Producer
and Moderator for Fan Fest's Walker Stalker Con

I met Jason when he moderated a panel session I participated in at a Walker Stalker Con focused on the topic of *Walking Dead*-inspired entrepreneurship. I had attended other sessions he moderated in the past and was always impressed with how comfortable he was on stage interacting with guests in an unscripted environment. I assumed he was a professional speaker or aspiring Chris Hardwick-style talk show host. When I learned that he was also an entrepreneur and a fantrepreneur, I reached out to him to discuss further.

Jason is a testament to the entrepreneurial model of "first to market." Launching his *Walking Dead*-themed podcast more than two months before *TWD* series first premiered on television, and then landing *TWD* series favorite Steven Yeun, a.k.a. Glenn, as an early guest, long before the character met an eye-popping death in season seven at the hands of Negan. But these early wins allowed his podcast to break out from the noise and continue to attract new fans, even as the TV show is about to enter its tenth season. Jason credits the longevity of his podcast to strong production values, interesting guests, and keeping the show fast-moving so that the fun is infectious for the audience. A subtle pun.

I admitted to him that while I had been interviewed on many podcasts for my prior books and enjoyed participating and talking with the hosts—primarily because they are uncensored, meaning you can curse, which I am prone to do—I had never once listened to an entire show. I did not understand the podcast business model nor how people make money from it. He told me he uses Libsyn, and I replied that I use the generic version of that cholesterol lowering drug. He corrected me that Libsyn was Liberated Syndication, a network platform to host and publish podcasts.

He tried to educate me on the topics of media hosts, download statistics, and the monetization of listenership. Hosting entities provide podcasters a platform to post their podcasts for download, build websites and social media integration to promote the shows as well as track download and listener data. These stats can be shown to potential advertisers to bring them on board. The advertisers and podcasters can agree on a dollar value per one thousand anticipated downloads and are invoiced according to the actual results. Dollar values are capped to prevent any surprises for the sponsors, so they can plan for maximum marketing spending each month. Jason credits crowdfunding sites like Patreon with allowing new entrants into the field to test the waters and see if they can raise

enough interest and funding before they make larger investments in a podcast.

He expanded his reach by establishing a membership-
only Facebook page for fans dedicated to his show. A monthly
subscription allows them to interact with the podcast hosts as
well as each other. He is hoping to see a marriage proposal stem
from the group. While no nuptials thus far, the private page has
been used to arrange purely platonic gatherings at cons.

He further engages audiences by running contests and
recruits new sponsorships by approaching companies he finds
interesting. I asked him how he planned to scale his business
and he replied that he would read my book when released to give
him some good ideas. I thanked him…as I am a black hole of
insecurities that is always looking for validation. He continued
to state his understanding that all things, even zombies, have
a natural life span. While he continues his podcasting and
moderating duties with a focus on *TWD*, he has also dedicated
more of his time on growing on his own Podcastica brand.

"I cannot plan it all out, I just can't live that way."

—DAVE SOLO, *CEO of Walker Nation LLC, podcast*

Dave Solo is well known to fans of *TWD*, and while he's
a fan of the show, he does not credit it as his sole reason for
becoming a fantrepreneur. Rather, he considers it the blasting
cap that put in motion his most notable successes to date.

It seems that a *Walking Dead* future was rooted in his past,
having grown up three houses down from a cemetery, he too
was exposed to the zombie genre at way too early an age. He
recalled to me the story of his older sister taking him as a young
child to see the film *Dawn of the Dead*. I told him about my
experience where my older sister allowed me to sit with her to
watch *Children Shouldn't Play with Dead Things*. I had never

met Dave in person, but our grade school introductions to these non-age-appropriate films and the resulting trajectories of our lives are eerily similar. We came to the realization of one obvious, universal truth: that older sisters are evil to their younger brothers.

Evil older sisters aside, our entrepreneurial paths also were similar. Dave started his family young, and as such, wanted to keep his feet planted firmly on the ground when it came to starting new ventures.

The Walker Nation podcast was not his first fantrepreneurship, having launched one while only in high school. He ran a cable access show dedicated to professional wrestling, a fan base that shares many similarities with *TWD* following. He was a fan of the show and like many others, created a podcast to share his thoughts on each episode with friends. Soon, friends he had not told about the show contacted him to let him know they had discovered it on their own. Following that, he was contacted by fans that he had never met who were listening in from around the globe.

He formed Walker Nation LLC and trademarked the name for protection against any unforeseen liability. As the podcast listenership grew, he knew he needed to find corporate sponsors. In this digital world, while promoting his digital medium, Dave decided to approach his potential sponsors in a very old school, analog fashion. He began knocking on doors. "Nothing can substitute meeting someone in person, looking them in the eye and shaking their hand," he advised.

He approached companies that are well known within the pop culture community, who receive a thousand requests for podcast support a month, and he succeeded at winning their business by showing up at their door. He was a person in their office, not an email in their inbox. As Woody Allen once said, "Eighty percent of life is showing up."

He admits he had, and still has, his fair share of rejections. "As time goes by, the losses don't sting any less, but the victories feel better and better." he said. As his audience grew, he achieved exposure to new opportunities, and upon meeting Jason Cabassi, he became a Walker Stalker panel moderator. After a couple successful years of working with the conference, he moved on to work for Universal Orlando. I asked him about his plans for the future of his business, and his response was quite Zen.

"Let's see where this takes me," he said. "I don't always need a plan. If you told me a couple years ago that I would have a podcast with tens of thousands of listeners and be on a stage in London, England with *The Walking Dead* stars Norman Reedus and Andrew Lincoln, I would not have believed you. Ultimately, I am just a guy with a podcast and media past, the rest was hard work, respect, and ambition, and that is how I got to where I got. I cannot plan it all out, I just can't live that way."

CHAPTER SIX

DRAWING THE DEAD

"I realized right then—I had painted my last fish."
—SCOTT SPILLMAN, *Artist, Illustrator,*
Fan Festival Organizer

There are many amazing artists who use *TWD* and its cast of characters as their muse. Each approaches their medium with their own twist. I have seen one artist at cons who is known for painting his works frantically using both hands at one time, to the beat of pulsating music. Some artists use vibrant colors, while others have become well known for the sketching of characters, both living and dead, in only a black and white medium. Some artists create complex tributes to the show, encapsulating an entire season on one canvas, with themes woven throughout and hidden Easter eggs within the painting, that make you want to analyze each of their works as if you are investigating the Da Vinci Code.

I spoke with artist Scott Spillman, a fan favorite at Walker Stalker as well as other conventions. Unlike some of the other fantrepreneurs I interviewed, *The Walking Dead* was not his catalyst for becoming an artist but did alter the trajectory of his career. Scott was painting fine art, displayed and sold through galleries. Residing in Florida, he displayed and sold his paintings only in local galleries. He painted what appealed to the local Floridian aesthetics...which was sea life. His focus was fish and sea turtles, but felt he needed something more challenging to keep his skills fresh, to "sharpen the saw" as self-help author Stephen Covey said.

A fan of *TWD* and, in particular, the character Michonne, he read in the paper that the actress Danai Gurira, who plays the sword-wielding character, was going to be signing autographs at a local event. He painted her portrait with the anticipation that he would get her to sign it and hang it on his own wall. As he finished the piece, he himself was taken by how well it came out, and he created twenty-five prints of the original work to bring along, thinking he may be able to sell one or two while walking around the show. He arrived and stood in line to get the Danai's autograph when people started asking him about his painting and if the prints were for sale. He soon sold the first, and then a second. He heard someone yelling to him from several rows over who then passed money along through the crowd. Within twenty minutes, he was sold out. At that point, he realized he had painted his last fish.

His paintings take upwards of forty to sixty hours each to create, so he focuses on selling his lower priced prints of the originals. As this was a new market for him, he set out to promote his new line of work by joining every *Walking Dead* group on Facebook he could find. It was a new market and required a new mindset from how he had approached the gallery scene. He saw an immediate response, but after six months, he noticed his sales beginning to decrease. People loved his artwork, but once they hung it on the wall, there was no secondary use for it. So, he began printing his custom work on items used by the fanbase every day—coffee mugs, coasters, and mouse pads. He originally decided to outsource the merchandizing of products emblazoned with his art but feared that he could not control quality of what was produced and sold to the fan base. He made the investment in his own equipment to ensure high quality and consistency of all products that were printed with his art. With his painting and printing being run out of his house, and the US Postal Service picking up shipments from his front door, he realized that sometimes up to a week would go by without once stepping outside his door into the sunlight. As I wrote earlier, fantrepreneurship can be isolating.

Again, this was another fantrepreneur who was faced with the question of where to spend his time; either producing new art or running the business. As his artwork was so consuming, often taking over a week to create a single piece, he found he was creating less art than he wanted and was getting too caught up in the "everything else" of entrepreneurship. He had to do what all entrepreneurs do when they simply run out of hours in the day, they begin using up their hours at night. "You need to have that fire in the belly or you won't make it," he told me.

He had received his formal education in graphic and commercial arts, but after graduation, he would run into people from his class working retail and odd jobs. It was then that it hit him that to succeed in his chosen line of business, the artist needed more than just talent, they needed the absolute drive, the commitment, to give every bit of yourself to your craft...or it's not going to work. He began working more and more conferences on the weekends while painting every night. As his body of work grew, so did his following, and he began exhibiting at cons overseas. He grew his social media presence and began interacting more with fans, as he knew they were not just buying the art...they were buying the artist.

I asked him about something I had observed at fan conventions: novice artists walking around the show with their portfolio in their hand, looking to get feedback on their work from more established artists. He stressed that this was not the best way for a budding fantrepreneur to receive critical and useful feedback. When an artist is at the show, he has invested a lot just to be there. The cost of the booth, the travel, and the transportation of all the works. The show is meant for selling and promoting your work. He suggests artists meet him at the show and arrange for future conversations about evaluating their art. Scott is also providing new venues for artists to display their projects by establishing his own *Walking Dead-*inspired events.

CHAPTER SEVEN

(FUND)RAISING THE DEAD

"When there's no more room in hell, the dead will walk their dogs."

—*Anthony and Deann Muzikar,*
Philanthropists, Founders of Dog Walk of the Dead

This couple's story is different from others throughout the book. First, because their goal is not to make any money, but to raise money for others. Also, they did not set out to specifically begin a long-term venture, but simply host a one-time event. Anthony and Deann are fans of not only *The Walking Dead* but also of walking their dogs. They observed a trend while attending zombie walks; turns out, they were not alone in bringing their pets to participate in the fun.

They first got the idea in 2011 while attending New Jersey's massive Asbury Park Zombie Walk, an event that has broken the Guinness Book of World Records twice. They noticed people incorporated their dogs into their zombie cosplay, so the following year, they organized a zombie walk that was dedicated to zombie dogs. Already having a relationship with the local animal shelter, they decided to establish the event as a fundraiser. The first Dog Walk of the Dead was scheduled to coincide with Halloween, and upon word spreading, others began offering live music, concessions, and prizes for costume contests. Suddenly, this little fundraiser became an "event." Over eight hundred people showed up and all the money was donated to the animal rescue shelter.

They thought they were done, but the dead kept pulling them back in. The following year, they began receiving inquiries about the next zombie dog walk. Realizing the turnout would probably be larger the second year than the first—which was already much larger than expected—they realized they needed to find a bigger venue to hold it. They also became more organized in their promotions and methods of donations. Six years and six events later, they hold the event in a donated fairground that has both indoor and outdoor facilities to hold all the participants, observers, vendors, and—of course—dogs.

They accept no income from the organization. This is a sacrifice, as even though the event is held one day a year, the planning, organizing of fundraising, and promotion of the event continues all year long. They rely heavily on the donated time and efforts of friends, and the local shelters cover the costs of flyers and posters. The artwork that goes into the annual flyers is also donated. One year, a local brewer donated small backpacks and they canvassed local businesses and other fantrepreneurs to donate items for fundraising raffles. They credit the success of the event to aligning themselves with well-known animal charities and holding the event on the same date every year. The support of local radio stations and media outlets help spread the word, so as not to incur advertising costs. The Dog Walk of the Dead motto is to do as much as they can for as cheap as they can.

"I love it, I love every part of it," Anthony told me. "So, the time I spend working on the event does not feel like work at all. It feels like my life."

And the donations and support keep growing. When it comes to dogs and cats, no one says no.

"I'm an ordinary guy who came up with an idea supported by extraordinary people."

—*Joe Ripple, Founder of Scares that Care*

Another such horror-themed philanthropy is Scares that Care. Founded in 2007 by Joe Ripple, a retired police detective, the charity serves as a continuing tribute to the daughter of a fellow officer who had succumbed to a terminal illness.

Joe had been hired as head of security for a weekend horror conference that was taking place locally. He was not involved in that community but was immediately impressed by the fandom he observed. Not knowing what to expect from people who attended a conference focused on horror, he was taken aback by how nice and kind the horror fan attendees were. A community of ordinary, yet very dissimilar, people were coming together with one thing in common. Although not a horror junkie himself, he began working other similar cons and got the sense of a tribal community feeling, seeing the same attendees repeatedly.

He founded Scares that Care based upon that community. He credits his background in law enforcement with giving the charity early credibility and within two years of forming, they had raised and donated $10,000 to a children's charity. In 2011, Scares became an IRS-approved 501(c)(3) nonprofit—allowing contributors to enjoy the tax benefits of their donations, which leads to larger and more frequent donations. "We refocused to fight the *real monsters* of childhood illness, burns and breast cancer by helping families that are experiencing these extraordinary hardships cope with the financial burden," Joe shared with me.

I asked Joe about his philosophy on running his business, and he explained: "Everyone has a voice in our organization, from the board of directors, to the CEO, to the people in the field. It is important to recognize not only the people who donate, but the staff of sixty-five volunteers who help run the charity."

Joe told me that not everyone he has encountered has been on board with a horror-based charity. He recounted one story where he was on the check outline of a grocery store, wearing his "Scares that Care" t-shirt. The cashier asked him about it and he gave her the quick synopsis. A woman standing behind him expressed her disapproval, accusing him of using horror and fear to raise money for children. Joe handed her his card as CEO of the charity, and when she asked what he expected her to do with it, he replied she should hang on to it. If she was ever in need of their charitable foundation, she should call him, and he promised he would never judge her the way she judged him.

CHAPTER EIGHT

MOLDING THE DEAD

"The secrets I use to create my best works have come from my prior failures."

—DAVE NAGY, *Founder of Dave's Dark Realm*

One of the most interesting fantrepreneurs I met was Dave Nagy, whose path to business ownership was far from typical but encompassed all the ideas of true entrepreneurship.

Dave was not a Harvard or Wharton School of Business graduate. He was not a business major in college, nor did he ever attend college. Dave was an auto mechanic who found himself unemployed after his garage had a round of layoffs. Assuming he would soon be called back to work, he spent his time finding ways to fill his day. On a lark, he visited a psychic who gave him the cryptic prediction that he would soon see his artwork overseas. While he did enjoy drawing for fun, he had no ambition for career in any form of the arts. As the fall arrived, and being a fan of Halloween, he began working at a local haunted house. He observed the rubber props and creepy prosthetics that resembled body parts used at the attraction, and in a conversation with its owner, was surprised to hear how much the man had paid for the latest rubber replicas. He researched the market online and found other suppliers of the products, but they too sold horror-related items that were equally as costly. He set out to try and see if he could meet the quality of these products and provide them to his boss at the haunted house for lower costs.

He began tinkering around in his garage with latex and cotton, and soon molded his first severed hand. He was disappointed by the quality of the outcome. A molding error had caused the hand to be misshapen. Still, he decided to post a picture of his first creation online just to see what his friends thought. One of his friends was so intrigued by the piece that she offered to buy it. He agreed, and when he began to create the shipping label, he realized he would be shipping his piece of art from his studio in New Jersey to his friend, who now lived in Norway. The soothsayer's prediction had come true and given birth to Dave's Dark Realm.

He took sculpting lessons and researched how to create latex molds online. He wanted to research everything he could about this business. "I want to know everything. I have lost a lot of sleep on the things that I knew I didn't know." He continued to improve upon his work, though he told me he never feels he will find perfection. His business grew as he began selling his products to local haunted houses and amateur film makers. He created a line of body parts that resembled and displayed horrific injuries, and showcased them at local horror cons.

He would draw attention to his display by crafting a movie-quality zombie mask and adopting the persona of Zombie Dave at the con, and he remains in character, demonstrating complete "commitment to the bit" throughout all exhibit show hours. His adoption of a completely different persona while working his booth has served multiple beneficial purposes. First, it draws people's attention to his booth. His zombie make-up, morbid facial prosthesis, and physical mimicking of a *Walking Dead* Walker has made him and his booth a popular destination for selfie-taking attendees. Second, the costume and alter-ego identity allow him to overcome any innate shyness or hesitancy about approaching people cold in order to promote his business. In fact, his costume transforms him into a walking promotional billboard for his wares.

"I do this because I want to," Dave told me, "as the costume puts me at ease when I am at a show, as well as drives business to my booth. But also, I am a fan, and I want other fans to have the best possible time while attending the con. This helps me feel like I am contributing."

In our discussion, he began to lament that he wished he had started this entrepreneurial path twenty years earlier. I told him to wipe those regrets from his mind. He began his business when it was supposed to have begun. I harkened back to his tale about visiting the psychic, and while I do not believe she had any real foresight into the future, I do believe Dave had come to the perfect confluence of circumstances that led him to be successful. Twenty years earlier, he was not laid off and looking for something to keep him active, the show and comic *The Walking Dead* had not yet been written, and the prevalence of social media was not yet there to allow him to showcase his very first creation and facilitate his first sale. It happened at that moment because there was no other moment in time it *could* have happened.

Before we ended our conversation, he expressed incredulity that I would want to interview him for this book. He relayed that he had only one employee and ran his business out of his garage—he was not running the Skywalker Ranch of special effects creation. He asked why anyone would care about his tiny micro-business. I explained to him that his story is so intriguing as it represented the perfect story of fantrepreneurship. He was placed into a circumstance through a layoff where he could have sat on the couch, complained about his misfortune and waited for someone else to give him a job. Instead, he used his time to find his own economic path forward, and without any formal training or a large chunk of personal wealth to dip into, he tinkered around with something that interested him, and created both a new business and a new product: a line of high-quality, low-cost horror props.

CHAPTER NINE

CON'ING THE DEAD

"After all, how much juice can you squeeze from Savior Number Four?"

—DAVE SOLO, *Walker Nation LLC*

As I mentioned before, I am a trade show-loving guy. As that is the business growth avenue I was knowledgeable about and comfortable with, I made it my primary marketing strategy for my fantrepreneurship focused on selling my zombie novels. I even enjoy the hours when I am there setting up my booth, either the morning of the show or the night before, as you can feel the energy building in the convention hall. Most of the vendors are super-fans as well, so there is always chatter and "horse trading" going on between exhibit booths. "I will trade you one of my books for your handmade necklace," and such.

When it gets closer to opening, the buzz from the vendors, the celebrities, the volunteers, the security, and the AV teams all starts becoming more frenetic. The music begins, like the disjointed, unharmonious sound of an orchestra tuning up before the curtain rises. As soon as the show floor doors open, the fans come flooding in. There is only one uniformity to con attendees, which is their shared fandom. Other than that, it is the most diverse gathering of people you will come across. All races, all ethnicities, all religions, all sexual orientations, all education levels, all income levels, and yet, all with at least one thing in common: their shared passion for the topic of the con.

As the event continues, a fan-created second life takes shape. A temporary community based upon that shared interest. At a time when eBay, Etsy, Amazon, and a million other websites offer all the art and entertainment your mind and soul could desire, people still travel hundreds of miles and pay sometimes ridiculous amounts of hard-earned income just to spend a day or two walking around a convention center that is usually too hot or too cold, shopping for that "only you would like that" item. It was while attending and then exhibiting at these cons where I became fully immersed within the fantrepreneurship universe and saw the potential micro-targeted marketing.

I have now been a vendor at Horror Con, Comic-Con, and Walker Stalker for five years. I've found that the professional business tracts I established in the conference circuit— consumer goods, technology, and defense—differ only slightly from the pop culture-themed cons. When it comes to the larger entertainment events, such as the New York City and San Diego Comic-Cons, the lines blur even further due to the presence of larger corporations and media empires, businesses with much deeper pockets for con presence than the average fantrepreneur.

I enjoy the camaraderie offered at the cons, talking about pop culture topics with vendors and attendees, as I am someone who receives my energy through interacting with groups of people. I do understand though, for those that are not naturally social beings, that working the con circuit as a primary focus of your business plan can be overwhelming and exhausting. As I discussed earlier, for the entrepreneur that is an unaware introvert, or aware yet cannot find a coping process to force sociability, the con route will ultimately prove frustratingly and inexplicably unsuccessful.

The typical fan attendee will spend a couple hours, and usually a couple hundred dollars, and then they are happy to get back to their normal lives. But others are not so eager to return to reality. They don't want to leave that one realm where there is an actual unity of community. There is an addictive quality along with a palpable energy created through the collective fandom of a convention. I have noticed that these fans will return the following year as vendor fantrepreneurs.

Entrepreneurs that focus on organizing these conferences take on a large amount of risk. Probably the most amount of exposure and investment of any other fantrepreneurship I have discussed thus far. They must cover the costs for the facilities, the paychecks of the staff, negotiate contracts with vendors, service companies, celebrity booking agents, and unions, and an endless number of other professionals who will have their hand out or looking to make a few dollars more. They are always at the mercy of weather and competing events. A con organizer is constantly trying to figure out where to hold that next event, and what theme or celebrity to center it around, without guarantee that it is going to work. Con organizers are often the target of social media attacks. Sometimes fair commentary, sometimes unwarranted. Blaming the organizer for a poorly organized, or poorly promoted show, or being slow to refund money from a cancelled event, is fair game. Blaming the con for a celebrity that cancels at the last moment, or for the price of an autograph or selfie with the star, is not. If Joe Shmoe is currently the hottest name in your genre of choice, the con and the celebrity will charge what the market will bear.

If you feel the prices are too much for you to bear, don't get the autograph. You will survive. Celebs have a limited shelf life, the actor that is hot today usually spent a decade or more working in obscurity. He may have served you coffee two years prior. As the talent, the show or film, and the genre are suddenly popular, their prices will skyrocket like any hot stock. A couple years later, they may be sitting in the vendor area, at a small locally organized con, signing movie still photos or headshots for twenty dollars. It is all cyclical, and as I said, based on the whims of fans.

But if this is a tract of business you want to base your fantrepreneurship upon, I again suggest volunteering for a larger con and trying to absorb as much as you can. Ask a million questions and consider answers the payment for your contribution of time and effort. The worst that can happen is they will get annoyed and not ask you back, but chances are, if your questions seem sincere and you are polite in posing them, the organizers will be responsive.

Then start off small, organizing a fan topic trivia night at a local bar, or a fan discussion at a comic book store. Find one or two of those third- and fourth-tier celebrities to come out. You won't get fans turning out to pay for their autographs; "After all," as I was once told, "How much juice can you squeeze from Savior Number Four?" But fans may be interested in hearing about their time on the set, and for a small fee, that actor will run the trivia game, or karaoke, or discussion group. Usually the bar or shop will offer the room at no charge in exchange for your promoting the event and drawing in a crowd on a normally slow night. It's a low-risk way of testing the waters if this is the path for you.

CHAPTER TEN

BOOKING THE DEAD

"I'm not really a 'fan' of the terms fantrepreneur."
—SEAN CLARK, Founder and CEO of Convention All Stars

Celebrities have agents, managers, and a myriad of other support people who ensure they are chosen for the best parts and get the best possible media attention. Entrepreneurs from around the country have found a way to get a taste of that Hollywood life by forming a new market segment, booking celebrities for photo and autograph sessions at pop culture-themed conventions. One of the most well known in this new industry is Sean Clark, CEO of Convention All Stars. Sean represents *The Walking Dead* fan favorites such as Norman Reedus (Daryl Dixon) and Jeffrey Dean Morgan (Negan).

"I'm not really a 'fan' of the terms *fantrepreneur* or *fanagers*," Sean Clark says. Sean does not sugar coat what he wants to tell you, which makes him perfect for his role in dealing with celebrities, those that book celebrities, and those that are fans of celebrities. Once I asked him jokingly if he would become my agent and make me famous. "Nope!" he replied. "You gotta be famous before I represent you."

Established in 2005, the company has grown to become one of the leaders in personal appearance representation. His company had its break out moment in 2012 when actress Jamie Lee Curtis, a horror icon, decided to do her one and only convention appearance.

Convention All Stars has grown to a staff of over twenty people and represents close to three hundred celebrity clients, including a majority of *TWD* and *Fear the Walking Dead* cast members. His business keeps him constantly on the road, and the universal appeal for both the show and the actors has allowed him to travel worldwide with the cast and experience passion and fandom from many cultures.

Sean's business is based purely on fandom, and as such, needs to continually keep up with a show or a character's popularity. Identification of who and what is currently hot, as well as keeping an eye on emerging stars who will be a future convention all-star, is what will keep his business on top and in demand.

But this business, as do all, comes with unexpected challenges that are nearly impossible to anticipate. If your business involves bringing together fans with their favorite *Walking Dead* celebrity for photo ops, you probably would not have thought you needed to inform the fans that while they may pretend to be a biter, it is not okay to *actually* bite the celebrity. Yes, that really happened.

Of all entrepreneurial tracks I have listed in this book, this one is the hardest to break into. Your product is people. Not just normal people, but people who are very hard to get in touch with, people who are going to be wary of strangers, and people who most likely have prior booking agents. Unless you have a pre-existing relationship with the celebrities or a reputation for working with all the large conventions, you most likely could not just step into this field. But if you want to investigate this field more, I would suggest volunteering at a local con. Many of the events offer opportunities for volunteers, which allows you access into the con at no charge. But keep in mind that you will be working most of the time, will usually be put on the most boring assignment your first couple of times, and never know ahead of time where you will be stationed. Volunteers who have proven themselves to behave in a professional manor—meaning they show up on time, do as they're asked, stay at their station, and don't act weird around the celebrities—will find themselves in better and better positions.

One of the most coveted is that of escorting the celebs from the holding area to their signing tables. The con and the celeb both make their money by charging for pictures and signing autographs. As the star walks through the show floor, they can be swamped with fans seeking freebies. But the star is not the one who lets the fan down by saying no to the fan's request, they leave that to the handlers who politely crush the fans' dreams and tell them to go pay and stand in line like everyone else. Those soul crushers are usually volunteers. Another position allows the volunteer to sit next to the star and keep track of the pictures signed and photos taken. These stations allow the volunteer to get an up-close look at part of what goes into the celebrity booker's role. If the star is chatty, the volunteer may find themselves spending the day kibitzing with a film or TV star. If the star is grumpy that day, best to keep quiet and focus on your assigned task. Another tract would be to offer volunteered time directly to the bookers to learn more about their industry. Before you pursue this industry, I would strongly suggest renting the Peter O'Toole film *My Favorite Year* or the more recent Russell Brand/Jonah Hill film *Get Him to the Greek*.

CHAPTER ELEVEN

CONSUMING THE DEAD

"My focus at conventions is always on the unique products or services that you can't find anywhere else."
—JENICE CELEBRE, *Fan of TWD Fantrepreneurs*

I wanted to find out more about why fans choose some vendors over another, especially with the wide variety of arts, literature, and services they have to choose from on the vendor floor. Attending a con is not cheap. Besides the entry price, many fans travel from across or even out of state, which comes with all the associated costs of a vacation. How does a vendor stand out, especially if they are providing a product or service that may have multiple competitors? Some shows are so crowded with illustrators, painters, and Funko POP! sellers, that you couldn't swing a dead cat without hitting one. Of course, in this realm, that dead cat will soon reanimate and eat you alive…but that's another story.

I received the below email from Elizabeth Jones, another vendor whom I had met at a Walker Stalker Con. She recounted her own path towards fantrepreneur:

> *I am a stay at home mom to three kids and live in Exeter, NH. I am a cake decorator and formed my own company called Cakes by Elizabeth. I do everything from my home, I am all self-taught, and love creating cakes! I love having creative freedom to have fun decorating.*
>
> *I attended my first Walker Stalker Con in 2014 in Boston, MA. It was such an amazing time and was my first convention experience. While there I had noticed a vendor had a large tiered cake on display and thought it would be awesome to sell my own baked goods at the convention someday.*
>
> *Following the convention, I reached out to one of the staff members to inquire about how I could support the conference. They told me the show was looking for a baker to donate their time and talents to make cakes for celebrity guests at Walker Stalker Con in exchange for free attendance at the con and a chance to meet the stars of the show. I volunteered, and since 2015 I attend each Walker Stalker in Boston and New Jersey.*

In 2018, Elizabeth began selling her cakes and baked goods at her own booth. She proudly displays photos of herself posing with stars Emily Kinney, Ming Chen, Michael Cudlitz, Tom Payne, Bruce Campbell, IronE Singleton, Ross Marquand, as well as her custom, fandom-inspired, baked creations.

I also spoke to *Walking Dead* fan and frequent conference attendee Vickie Poisseroux about what draws her to certain vendors and artists. Besides the artists' talents and, of course, her personal tastes, it is her interactions with the artists that keeps her coming back to their booths year after year. She spoke about artists such as Rob Prior and Corey Smith as well as others, who make time to spend just talking to her, her daughter, and other attendees. Both Vickie and Elizabeth expressed how much the personal interaction between vendor and customer resonated with them.

Finally, I received the below email from Jenice Celebre, a frequent con attendee and moderator of *Walking Dead* fan groups that allow members to coordinate meeting each other at upcoming events:

> *I have been a diehard fan of the zombie genre for a very long time.*
>
> *My focus at conventions is always on the unique products or services that you can't find anywhere else. While it is very tempting to buy every* Walking Dead *or horror figurine, DVD, poster, etc. what I tend to purchase are the personalized products from artists, including custom-made jewelry with memorable images from the* Walking Dead.
>
> *I have found vendors who made Christmas zombie ornaments, which as a fan, was a must for our tree. The cons are my family's favorite past time. As crazy as we may seem to a non- horror or con-attending person, attendees are the most amazing, caring, and kind people you can ever meet.*

Those artists and vendors are happy to pose for pictures and follow up by adding "likes" and comments when tagged in fans' posted pictures of themselves alongside the artist's work. Such

interpersonal experiences are beneficial for both fan and entrepreneur, as they facilitate word-of-mouth revenue and are the
foundation for a lifelong customer. Simple pleasantries such as
greeting a returning customer, or the return of an email, seem
trivial…yet are essential. While this advice may seem rudimen-
tary and perhaps condescending to some reading this book,
you would be surprised at how many new and established business are managed by people whose rudeness to customers and
fans, either purposeful or unintended, has stifled their success.

Positive and ongoing interaction with fans and customers
should not begin only when the show hours start, and like-
wise, should not end when the show is over. Your social media
strategy should include posting pictures of yourself with
customers, fans, and other vendors after the event, ensuring
you tag them while doing so. Also, reaching out to prior fans
and customers in the weeks leading up to a show to remind
them you will be attending.

Your social media strategy should to be thought-out and
consistent. I cornered the market on the term "ExitZero-
Zombie." It is my website URL, my Twitter and Instagram
handle, my Facebook page, and my email address. These
are simple and inexpensive ways to achieve messaging and
brand consistency.

Your social media strategy should include sharing just a bit
of personal information about yourself, as fans want to know
more about the artists and businesses they spend their money
with. It should not include oversharing or be a platform where
you feel the need to share every pondering or opinion. As we
said earlier, share just enough to keep people informed and to
promote your business, but not enough to get into trouble.
I wish I could provide more specific guidance on what you
should and should not post, but that would be impossible.
All I can suggest is that if you do not have the self-control

to handle social media, it is best to not use it at all or have someone else manage it for you. Otherwise you can stay away from promoting online and use the postal service. That is not a joke. I know it is more expensive than emails, but honestly, how many emails do you get a day versus letters you receive a week? (And I am not including bills.) I can also advise if you are self-aware enough to recognize that you have no behavioral self-control, you may want to consider an entrepreneurship venture in reality TV.

CHAPTER TWELVE

AROUSING THE DEAD

*"I could not imagine my world if I were not a
true horror fan."*

—MEOWSTRESS, *Poisonous Pinup and Horror Hostess*

Some fantrepreneurs focus on aesthetics to which they know the fan base will respond. The growth of companies devoted to beautiful, barely dressed "alternative models" has made this a fantrepreneurial area that has become, forgive the pun, fully engorged. Major players and companies such as Suicide Girls, which featured tattooed and pierced young women, led to more targeted, horror-themed modeling sites such as Bloody GOREgeous, GOREgous Girls, and Poisonous Pinups. This brand of "horrotica" features alt models bathed in blood, mimicking famous horror movie scenes, and reanimating the dead art of burlesque in live performances.

The business model from these ventures is relatively straightforward and no different from any business featuring eye-catching beauties. Subscription magazines, websites, custom photo shoots, and promotional videos are the delivery mechanism; however, the true dollar value is derived from other companies willing to pay for associated advertisements within the magazines and websites.

Other models are independent and have created their own following and sell their own photos and custom shoots to their self-generated fanbase. Applications such as Instagram and Snapchat and content sharing websites like MagCloud, Patreon, and DeviantArt, create platforms for horror models to enter the world of entrepreneurship with very limited capital investment.

In speaking with these companies and models, they consider themselves to be artists, influencers, and horror hostesses and enthusiasts; however, they are not pursuing the fetish community, which is an entrepreneurial tract of its own. Some have more traditional modeling portfolios alongside their ghoulish girl works, but others have established themselves as solely involved in horror. I spoke to one of the Poisonous Pinups named Meowstress, who had just graced the cover of their latest magazine. "For me, horror was in my blood, as growing up, my mother was a horror fanatic." she told me. She had her break when cast by Troma Entertainment to appear in a horror film, and later invented the Meowstress persona, appearing as a horror-themed pinup girl. Meowstress does not see herself as an alternative model, or a model at all, but rather following in the footsteps of famous horror hostesses such as Vampira and Elvira.

CHAPTER THIRTEEN

IMPERSONATING THE DEAD

"To succeed you need to learn how dust tastes."
—CHRIS TWELLMANN, *The German Abraham*
and CEO of Abraham's Army

Unlike most cosplayers, Chris Twellmann does not need to do much to present himself as a carbon copy of the character Abraham from *The Walking Dead*, played by the actor Michael Cudlitz. Most days, he does not need to do more than roll out of bed. Same face, same eyes, same hair and same mustache, yet surprisingly, it was not Chris who first noticed the resemblance.

Distance could have played a role in that. Chris was born, raised, and still residing in Germany when *TWD* was taking America by storm. But, just like a virus, the fandom of a great show cannot be contained by international borders, and soon it was a global presence. Chris was working in the marketing department of a large law firm when one of his coworkers posted a picture of him on Facebook with the caption "Our own German Abraham." The photo went viral and even Chris embraced his new-found doppelgänger status. He first began playing up the resemblance in Germany, tweaking his hair so that it more closely resembled the character, and sometimes donning the military style clothing worn by the fictional sergeant.

It was after his first visit to a Walker Stalker event in America that Chris realized the scope of the opportunity and relocated himself from Germany to ground zero of Walker fandom: Senoia, GA.

I had so many "off the topic of this book" questions I wanted to ask him, such as if the actors ever got annoyed with cosplayers who hit the genetic lottery of being an actor's carbon copy, or if anyone had approached him to live out their Abraham fantasy, and to what lengths he would go to continue the resemblance. For instance, if the actor Cudlitz—whose character on the show is now deceased—re-emerged in a new franchise just as popular, only with a head shaved clean as a cue ball, would Chris head to the barber?

But I kept my questions focused on the subject at hand— how Chris had parlayed his resemblance into a business lucrative enough to move to a new country. Chris had been in marketing for twenty-five years and had spent ten of those as a creative director, so he was experienced enough to recognize a business market that had potential. He also had served as a staff sergeant and paratrooper in the German Army, so he knew there was no gain without risk and, as he re-quoted a prior mentor, "To succeed you need to learn how dust tastes."

He opened a photo studio in his adopted town and re-created backgrounds from iconic scenes that featured the Abraham character. He began charging for photos, as well as crafting his own line of handmade, self-designed merchandise.

"You have to decide how much you can afford to lose before you begin to gain."

—CECIL GARNER A.K.A. CECIL GRIMES,
Actor, Film Maker, Pioneer of SetPlay

It all started with no-shave November. He had let his beard and mustache grow out, and his fellow colleagues at the mortgage banking firm noticed his resemblance to *The Walking Dead*'s Sheriff's Deputy Rick Grimes, played by actor Andrew Lincoln. Not really noticing the resemblance himself, he decided to let his hair and beard to grow out.

Often a person cannot recognize their own destiny until it is staring them right in the face. When Cecil Garner, now known as Cecil Grimes, first met Andrew Lincoln, the two stared each other in the face. Cecil admits, the experience made him become dizzy. "We both just stood there, examining each other's face, as if we were looking into a mirror," he said.

By this time, he had already won an international Rick Grimes look-a-like contest and had progressed from showing up at cons as an attendee in off-the-shelf cosplay and had made the leap to fantrepreneur and pioneer of SetPlay. He recalled for me his first experience at a *Walking Dead* convention. He had purchased an Officer Grimes costume from a Spirit of Halloween pop-up store at a local mall. Upon arrival at the con and entering the exhibit hall, he did not make it more than ten feet before he was stopped and spent the next several hours taking selfies. It was years later, after he had invested a considerable amount of money into cosplaying the Grimes character and creating elaborate sets for cons, that he first met the reclusive actor Andrew Lincoln. Lincoln rarely attends fan conventions, appearing at, at most, two shows a year. There is little chance of spotting him around the set or in town during shoots, as he flies back home to the UK at the end of each shooting schedule. So, for most fans, Cecil Grimes was as close as they were going to get to Rick Grimes, and they embraced him as a welcome consolation prize.

Cecil was one of the pioneers of "set play." While both professional and amateur cosplayers have been mimicking *TWD* characters at cons since the show premiered, Cecil was the first to bring full recreations of major sets to the convention floor. The backdrops were elaborate, taking up to eleven hours to load into the convention hall and set up. Sixteen-foot towers simulating the prison guard tower or Alexandria Safe Zone lookout tower loomed over the vendor hall, drawing visitors over to his photoshoot business and allowing fans to up their selfie game. He had no set design experience and visited Home Depot more times than he can count, but within seven days—the same amount of time it took God to create the universe—Cecil had created his first *TWD* set: an authentic looking reproduction of the prison. With innovation comes investment. He needed to purchase not just the materials to build the set, but high-end cameras, lighting equipment, printers, ink, and a vehicle large enough to transport the massive display. He had invested thousands of dollars. "You have to decide ahead of time how much you are willing to lose before you gain," he said.

While imitation is the sincerest form of flattery, entrepreneurs don't pay their bills with flattery. "The first year I did this, I was the only one. The second year, I saw one other vendor attempt to mimic set play set up. By the third year there were five and by the fourth year, I counted seven, but by then the shows were so large with *Walking Dead* fans that I rarely had a chance to leave my booth," Cecil explained.

Unlike many fantrepreneurs, who are at most a two or three-person shop, Cecil's business requires a full staff. He hires other costumed actors, photographers, and staff to print the photos, take the money, and install and remove the large set. People are the largest expense, as he needs to cover their pay for the show, including their travel and hotel rooms. Also, employees bring risk, as travel and set install always comes with the chance of injury, so liability insurance is needed. "I needed to keep innovating and creating new designs of my SetPlay so that I stood out from the others and kept my customers' loyalty from con to con. By this time, the shows were so crowded, I had repeat customers seeking me out for photos, and even with my sky-high tower, not be able to locate my booth. By the time they did, they had already paid for another set play photo-op. It was frustrating, but if you have the passion, you will find the path forward."

For this type of business, investments are not singular, onetime costs, but recurring expenses. Ink, paper, and other consumables of the service are always being purchased. The set needs to be updated to reflect the changing storyline of *TWD*. Even his own personal appearance needs to change to reflect the onscreen character's growth. And with all this continued investment, there is no guarantee of continued success. "After all, I have now been doing this for years, and last season, the Rick Grimes character left the original series. My worry is how long will people pay to take a picture of a guy who looks like a guy who used to be on a show?"

I asked him about how he planned to scale his business, and his response was very interesting. He had tried to add more merchandise to his current offering, which consisted of the customer posing with him on the mock-up set and walking away with a color 8x10. He added additional items to sell, such as miniature Lucille bats (Negan's weapon of choice) as well as other tchotchkes. This did not work out well and slowed the flow of customers. Customers began taking too long deciding if they wanted to purchase the additional items, which held up the line and caused other customers, who were waiting to purchase the more income-generating photos, to walk away.

Sometimes in entrepreneurial ventures less is more, and too many options can cause a decrease in sales. All entrepreneurs experience trial and error, and this was an important lesson for Cecil to focus on the core and most profitable product of the business.

So, he eliminated the additional items and created an improved web-based store, where photo takers can download digital versions of their pic with "Rick" as well as get the photos printed on coffee mugs and other items. Fantrepreneurship is a continuing cycle of trying new things to grow customers and revenue.

Cecil has not yet seen a slowdown of interest though. He is now a "Featured Guest" at most cons, which means the show organizers treat him not much different than if he were one of *TWD* cast. His booth and sometimes even travel expenses are covered, which increases return on investment for cons, but he still needs to cover the costs of his staff, consumables, and other expenses. His business has taken him worldwide, including Japan, Peru, and Europe. Fandom is an international language. His advice to others who want to pursue cosplay as their road to fantrepreneurship, market test your idea first. Go to cons and gauge the reaction of fellow fans.

The author can attest to this advice. When I first began attending horror cons to understand the lay of the land, I met Lou Avilleira, who had invented his own cosplay character called Father Evil. He wore a gothic looking priest's outfit, and was equipped with his own soundtrack, playing ominous sounding music. At that time, he was at the phase of showing up as a fellow attendee, happy to bask in the glow of fellow attendees' attention and requests for pictures. He and I got to talking after meeting a couple times and I asked him where he wanted to go with his concept. He knew he wanted to pursue this as more than just a hobby but did not yet have a business plan. We talked about it more at each consecutive meeting and soon, he had his first vending stand, offering merchandise featuring the character he created, which now had thousands of followers due to his personal appearances and web presence. He had become a "horror personality."

CHAPTER FOURTEEN

TOURING THE DEAD

"People were traveling across the country to meet me on some random bridge."

—CARRIE SAGEL BURNS, *Atlanta Movie Tours*
and Big Zombie Tours

Not every town is as embracing of sudden celebrity that is thrust upon it once it is associated with a pop culture hit. Some towns are represented in movies, books, or television shows, yet never hosted a single day of filming or had a character from the show set foot on the streets. This is not so for Senoia, Georgia, which has seen many productions come and go, briefly converting theirs and neighboring towns into temporary studio lots. So many iconic scenes from *The Walking Dead* have been filmed around Senoia that the region has become a hotbed for destination tourism.

I spoke with Carrie Sagel Burns of Atlanta Movie Tours who runs several pop culture-themed tours, but none more popular than the four she has created that are dedicated to the dead.

Movie and TV sets are temporary structures. Built, torn down, and the parts are re-used for a future set. When fans come to an area where an iconic scene or entire season was filmed, they don't want to see just an empty field where an artificial structure once stood, or a storefront that was enhanced through long-ago removed artificial structures or added later to the scene after filming via CGI. They want to see the threads woven together and to feel if they are standing where their favorite actors once stood. This could be a costly endeavor for a town to create a façade that resembles the movie set. Luckily, the producers of *TWD* did not need to make too many changes to the scenic area and iconic locations such as Woodbury and Alexandria. In fact, the barn where Rick first meets the Governor and Merle meets his end are still standing, nearly identical in appearance to how it appeared on the show and welcoming to visitors.

Carrie stepped in to provide these touring fans a locally-based experience. Coming from an entrepreneurial family, Carrie did not want to work for a corporation in which she did not have a stake in ownership, and in 2012, she realized that locals who were even remotely associated with filming of the series—be it as an extra, a zombie, or a crew member—had become so hooked that they would find a way to weave it into any conversation. As pop culture fans came into town for long-running conventions such as Dragon Con, they would make pilgrimages to *TWD* locations.

Carrie had previously run location tours in New York City where fans wanted to see locations used in HBO's *Sex and the City* and *The Sopranos* and by now, she recognized her next location-themed tour. She and a friend sketched out the concept on the back of a napkin over dinner and two months later, her business was up and running. She launched by providing a week of media tours, attracting local news reporters, bloggers, and influencers. She hired locals who had landed extra roles or bit parts on the series to provide their own tales and experiences to the attendees. Ten days later, when she had her first public tour, it was sold out.

As she had no physical structure to run her business out of other than her home; the guides would meet their guests at random sites around town to kick off the tour. She marveled at how people would come in from halfway across the country just to take a tour that would begin on a random bridge in Georgia. To ensure the early success did not wane, she skillfully worked social media to promote the tours and provided outstanding service to ensure customer loyalty. They returned for future tours as the shows sites and storylines continued to grow and encompass more of the town.

Her success did not go unnoticed and AMC began offering tours of the studio lots, which was a zone that her tours had not previously covered. She sees the AMC hosted tours as complimentary though, not comparative, as it provides the tourists a more fully fleshed-out experience.

Large corporations create the content, but the true fandom experience comes from entrepreneurs. She credits her success as an entrepreneur as having a strong second-in-command, as few business owners can do it all by themselves. She has always hired people that are as committed to the business as she is and insists on transparency in running the venture, so that if she ever needs to take time away, she knows there is a second or third person within her group who can pick up and run the show. She has scaled her business to include new offerings but is not straying too far from her fandom roots. Her small business now offers corporate team-building events, allowing corporations to bring co-workers together for a fun zombie survival course. She is in the process of turning a replica of Dale's RV from the first season into an escape room and is focused on growing future entrepreneurs through educational outreach to schools, even building curriculums centered around the historical locations visited on her tours. As the entertainment industry continues to use the state for creating new pop culture powerhouses—such as the recent film *Black Panther*—Carrie sees the opportunity in Georgia for fan-based entrepreneurships to flourish.

> *"The corporations produce the content, but the fans recognize the opportunities."*
>
> —SCOTT TIGCHELAAR, *Former President of Riverwood Studio*

Another entrepreneur that looms large in the Senoia region is Scott Tigchelaar, past president of Senoia-based Riverwood Studio and land developer in the region that would become home to *TWD* production. While Scott was an entrepreneur long before the undead invaded Senoia, he was quick to recognize the popularity of the show and continues to invest in the business of the dead. His development company had built and still owns the land and buildings which served as the show's Alexandria Safe Zone, as well as the businesses on the main street of Senoia which once served as the realm of the Governor when it was known as Woodbury. As the show entered season two, the small town and surrounding areas became a site of pilgrimage for fans. The fans wanted to take a piece of the dead with them as they left, but AMC had not anticipated the merchandising potential of the show and had not produced officially licensed items.

Scott approached AMC about producing and selling officially licensed merchandise, but the studio was resistant. As I have spoken to entrepreneurs over the past year, I have come to realize that this is a common refrain. "While the large corporations manufacture the content that produces a legion of fans," Scott conveyed to me, "it is usually a fan-based entrepreneur that identifies the market opportunities."

AMC had approached Scott about utilizing one of the show's sets to host a party. As this type of event was outside the scope of the originally-signed property use agreement, Scott, ever the deal maker, seized the opportunity. Scott used a very Woodbury Governor-like tactic and allowed the studio to use the site for the party, on the condition that they allow him to begin selling approved *TWD* merchandise. They arrived at an agreement, and within two weeks, The Woodbury Shoppe was open. The small location, offering at the time only a limited choice of merchandise, became so popular that he had to hire security to man the door and prevent overcrowding. Not long after, Scott was approached by *TWD* originator Robert Kirkman and his business partner David Alpert who wanted to form a partnership to support the store and offer official Skybound merchandise. By 2013, the store had outgrown its original location and Scott opened a larger shop, still on Main Street, offering the official line of AMC and Skybound *Walking Dead* merchandise, as well as custom-created merchandise that had both *TWD* and Senoia themes, thus greatly expanding the purchasing options for fans. With new episodes and new comics in production, the release of a continuingly growing line of merchandise should always stock the shelves and continue to draw fans back to the business.

Scott's entrepreneurial adventure with *TWD* team was just beginning. The shop expanded to provide a coffee shop, named The Waking Dead, which led to the merchandising of its own brand of *The Waking Dead* coffee. It was there that two fans met and began talking about organizing fan gatherings, such as premier watch parties. Those conversations continued, particularly when one of them overheard a coffee barista referring to a gaggle of fans hanging around the coffee shop like stalkers hoping to spot someone from *TWD*. She had nicknamed these people "Walker Stalkers," and thus, a new convention was born.

In 2016, as Scott sat on his front porch—which happens to also be where primary filming of the Woodbury scenes takes place—he was approached by Greg Nicotero with the idea of opening a bar and restaurant in town that would be owned by Greg and Norman Reedus. A place for the cast, crew, and locals to enjoy a drink and a meal at the end of the shooting day. An existing restaurant owned by Georgia-based country singer Zac Brown was soon on the market, and Scott brokered the acquisition to bring about Nic & Norman's restaurant, a non-zombie-themed eatery that looks to franchise around the country. In a mind-bending case of synchronicity, the deal between Scott, Greg, and Norman was sealed while the three were taking part in a cruise organized by the Walker Stalker Convention, which originated in the coffee shop, which originated from *The Walking Dead*. Entrepreneurship is all about weaving the threads and connecting the dots to identify where the unmet demand resides.

In 2017, AMC officially purchased the studio where they filmed *TWD*, signaling the studio and the show have a lot more stories to produce. Scott credits the success of his entrepreneurial endeavors to the fanbase who have made the show a phenomenon and the town a tourist location. The mixture of a hit TV show, iconic scenes filmed in existing locations that are accessible to fans, and the desire for *TWD*-themed merchandise has provided a multitude of fantrepreneurial opportunities.

CHAPTER FIFTEEN

INKING THE DEAD

"You don't need to be the one with the most natural talent, you just need to outwork those that have it."
—CHRIS ROHALEY (CHRIS 51), *Tattoo Artist, Con Organizer, Author, Reality TV Star, founder of GeeksterInk*

Chris Rohaley did not seek out the dead—the dead found him. A serial entrepreneur, he had early on questioned why tattooing had to be confined to only store fronts and the occasional tattoo cons. His living canvases were requesting designs from pop culture, horror, and generally all things that would fall into the category of Geek. He and a few others were crafting a new market in pop culture-inspired tattoo designs, so Chris decided to take this team of artisans to the masses by creating and staring in the A&E reality show *Epic Ink*.

The show featured some of the best pop culture-focused talent in the skin art industry, each artist bringing their respective talents and vision. The success of the show led to more requests for personal appearances at cons. But Chris had organized some of the best pop culture tattoo talent in the world, so he decided that instead of going the solo route, he would bring the full show on the road and organized the GeeksterInk Legends Tour. He brought together the artistic talents and customer service the fans wanted, and delivered it at horror and pop culture cons, where the fans gathered. Using the platform of fan conventions proved successful and the tour had been ongoing for several years, when he was invited to bring his team of artists to Walker Stalker Con. He became immediately hooked, as he found that this con focused more on the fan experience than others. He grew out his roster of artists and created a more eye-catching exhibit area, complete with scaffolding and banners.

"You don't need a lot of money or education to be an entrepreneur...you need dedication; you need to spend the hours not the dollars. You don't need to be the one with the most natural talent, you just need to outwork those that have it," Chris told me.

Attendees were not the only clients he found at the cons, but celebrity guests would come by to get ink. Some of the stars preferred to get their work done privately, after con hours, but others, such as *TWD* and *The Punisher* star Jon Bernthal received their tattoos there in the booth in front of the fans.

The success of the show opened the door for Chris 51 to begin appearing at cons. "I took it a step further and created the GeeksterInk Legends Tour, where I personally recruited all of the best pop culture artists in the industry together and brought them to the fans."

Chris is eager to correct me that he is not exactly a fantrepreneur. "I am an artrepreneur! I do it for the art, not the money. I do it for the passion. When you are fueled by passion, you never run out of gas. When money is your only motivator you lose sight of why you started in the first place, and you will never go the extra miles it takes to succeed. I never asked myself what the risks were or thought of the words, 'what if?' You can't allow those words to exist unless they end with 'I don't'. If you don't try, then what happens…nothing. And nothing is the worst thing that can happen! If you are confident and believe in your product or service, it will show, and be contagious, and others will follow."

CHAPTER SIXTEEN

BURYING THE LIVING

"We cannot predict, but we can prepare."
　　—ROBERT VICINO, *Founder of Vivos Global Shelter Network*

Robert Vicino's Vivos Shelters is a business I will classify as "Dead-adjacent," meaning it was not derived from *The Walking Dead*. While he launched Vivos in 2008, the concept for Robert's business came to him in 1982, decades before even *TWD* comic series. But I found the company and business plan so unique, so inextricably tied to the apocalyptic genre, I had to include it.

Over the past decade Vivos has built and developed apocalypse survival shelters around the world, with current accommodations for more than ten thousand people. Vivos shelters are deep underground, fully self-contained complexes designed to survive or substantially mitigate virtually any threat scenario, including everything from a pole shift, supervolcano eruptions, solar flares, earthquakes, tsunamis, pandemics, asteroid strikes, the anticipated effects of Planet X/Nibiru, nuclear explosions, a reactor meltdown, biological or chemical disasters, terrorism, and even widespread anarchy. And, of course, the zombie apocalypse!

Robert credits obtaining the right skillsets, resources, and capital over many years as the keys that brought Vivos to reality. When he first conceived Vivos, he had no idea what to do or how to get started. Yet for three decades, he never let the spark die, and used that timespan to develop and prepare for this mission. He would spend hours a day voraciously reading and researching everything he could on the threats and how to survive them, to become an expert on both the problems and what he determined to be the solution.

"Let's recognize that many people have their three-day bug-out bag, but nowhere to bug out to. They'll head for the hills, the country, or the desert, but guess what, that's where everyone else will go as well, and they won't be prepared with a bag or supplies…so get ready to hand yours over. Whether you leave well in advance of an event, during or after, the key is to have a real shelter community solution to go to." Robert tells me. The Vivos goal was to accommodate one in every one million people on the planet. To build a massive complex for several thousand people and give away the spaces to those people I would not want to be down there without! A true cross-section of society including all races, religions, ages, and skillsets. I asked him to clue me in on his future plans for the business. His response, "Onward and downward, building as many shelters in as many countries as we can."

EULOGY

I have only scratched the surface of the type of fan-focused entrepreneurial opportunities. For this book I have met with tattoo artists and models. Companies that produce every useful, beautiful, horrific, and nonsensical item you can imagine—from unique, homemade bars of soap, jewelry, musical instruments, and handbags, to working, drivable replicas of iconic pop culture cars. The professional and amateur cosplayers have created their own circular sub-genre of entrepreneurs in the paparazzi who follow them from con to con, taking photographs and then selling them back to the cosplayers. The cosplayers then create subscription sites for fans to view and purchase these photos, which attracts new cosplayers into the field, who will be followed by new photographers, bloggers, vloggers, and podcasters. Fandom has perpetual momentum. Each person I interviewed for this book suggested I consider speaking to two other fantrepreneurs.

The delineation between entrepreneur and fantrepreneur is thin. I am not implying that the start-up venture focused on a line of neck ties or grandma's recipe for baked cookies does not contain the same sense of love and passion for that subject matter, it's just that those type of entrepreneurs are not founding their company based upon fandom. Of course, if they founded their cookie business based upon their love of the TV show *Cake Boss*, then I would have to reconsider their designation. But you get the point. Otherwise, this discussion could turn into six degrees of Kevin Bacon, and that is a fandom all its own.

I would like to hear about your fantrepreneurial ideas and what inspired them. Please reach out to me on any of my social media platforms (Twitter, Instagram, or Facebook) with Exit Zero Zombie in the title. #ExitZeroZombie

ABOUT THE AUTHOR

Neil A. Cohen has spent over thirty years in sales, marketing, and corporate growth. He received his undergraduate degree from The College of New Jersey and a graduate degree of Master of Business Administration from Marymount University, Virginia. Neil has been trained in Shipley federal business capture and proposal process and has worked for large multinational corporations, small business and entrepreneurial startup ventures. He has served as Director of Business Development for firms as diverse as consumer goods, lobbying, trade associations, technology firms, and defense contractors. He is a member of multiple business networking groups and has been a board member of several industry associations. He formed his LLC as a fantrepreneurial venture to promote his own book series, the Exit Zero Zombie trilogy: *Exit Zero*, *Nuke Jersey*, and *Zombie Democracy*, all published by Permuted Press/Post Hill.

This fantrepreneurship allowed him to shift from being merely a fan of *The Walking Dead* series to becoming a participant within the community, participating in Barnes & Noble book signings, appearing as a panel guest at *Walking Dead*, Horror and Comic conventions, and appearing on television as a "zombie genre expert." He followed his apocalyptic ambition of making a living from the dead. Over the years he has taken the time to meet with other such *Walking Dead*-inspired entrepreneurs and hear their stories and ambitions.

Neil wrote this book based on his experiences supporting artists, authors, and entrepreneurs grow their brand. He has assembled a compilation of interviews and success stories of those who also have also made the leap from passion to action, from fandom to income, and became a new type of entrepreneur: the fantrepreneur.

Neil lives outside Washington, DC, with his wife Vicki and two daughters Sasha and Hannah.

Discover more about this title:
https://businessisdead.com/

Learn more about the *Exit Zero* Zombie trilogy of books:
http://www.exitzerozombie.com
Facebook: *https://www.facebook.com/exitzerozombie*
Twitter/Instagram: *@ExitZeroZombie*

Order *Exit Zero:*
http://EZzombie.com

Order *Nuke Jersey:*
http://NukeJersey.com

Order *Zombie Democracy:*
http://Zombie-Democracy.com

PERMUTED PRESS
needs **you** to help

SPREAD (THE) INFECTION

FOLLOW US!

f | Facebook.com/PermutedPress
🐦 | Twitter.com/PermutedPress

REVIEW US!

Wherever you buy our book, they can be reviewed! We want to know what you like!

GET INFECTED!

Sign up for our mailing list at PermutedPress.com

PERMUTED
PRESS

KING ARTHUR AND THE KNIGHTS OF THE ROUND TABLE HAVE BEEN REBORN TO SAVE THE WORLD FROM THE CLUTCHES OF MORGANA WHILE SHE PROPELS OUR MODERN WORLD INTO THE MIDDLE AGES.

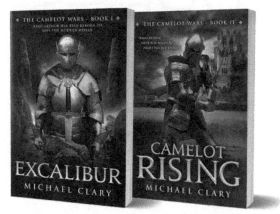

EAN 9781618685018 $15.99   **EAN** 9781682611562 $15.99

Morgana's first attack came in a red fog that wiped out all modern technology. The entire planet was pushed back into the middle ages. The world descended into chaos.

But hope is not yet lost— King Arthur, Merlin, and the Knights of the Round Table have been reborn.

THE ULTIMATE PREPPER'S ADVENTURE.
THE JOURNEY BEGINS HERE!

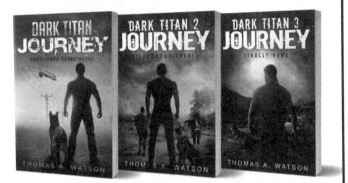

EAN 9781682611654 $9.99   EAN 9781618687371 $9.99   EAN 9781618687395 $9.99

The long-predicted Coronal Mass Ejection
has finally hit the Earth, virtually destroying
civilization. Nathan Owens has been prepping
for a disaster like this for years, but now he's
a thousand miles away from his family and
his refuge. He'll have to employ all his hard-won
survivalist skills to save his current community,
before he begins his long journey through
doomsday to get back home.

PERMUTED
PRESS

THE MORNINGSTAR STRAIN HAS BEEN LET LOOSE—IS THERE ANY WAY TO STOP IT?

An industrial accident unleashes some of the Morningstar Strain. The

EAN 9781618686497 $16.00

doctor who discovered the strain and her assistant will have to fight their way through Sprinters and Shamblers to save themselves, the vaccine, and the base. Then they discover that it wasn't an accident at all—somebody inside the facility did it on purpose. The war with the RSA and the infected is far from over.

This is the fourth book in Z.A. Recht's The Morningstar Strain series, written by Brad Munson.

PERMUTED
PRESS

GATHERED TOGETHER AT LAST, THREE TALES OF FANTASY CENTERING AROUND THE MYSTERIOUS CITY OF SHADOWS...ALSO KNOWN AS CHICAGO.

EAN 9781682612286 $9.99   **EAN** 9781618684639 $5.99   **EAN** 9781618684899 $5.99

From *The New York Times* and *USA Today* bestselling author Richard A. Knaak comes three tales from Chicago, the City of Shadows. Enter the world of the Grey—the creatures that live at the edge of our imagination and seek to be real. Follow the quest of a wizard seeking escape from the centuries-long haunting of a gargoyle. Behold the coming of the end of the world as the Dutchman arrives.

Enter the City of Shadows.

WE CAN'T GUARANTEE THIS GUIDE WILL SAVE YOUR LIFE. BUT WE CAN GUARANTEE IT WILL KEEP YOU SMILING WHILE THE LIVING DEAD ARE CHOWING DOWN ON YOU.

EAN 9781618686695 $9.99

This is the only tool you need to survive the zombie apocalypse.

OK, that's not really true. But when the SHTF, you're going to want a survival guide that's not just geared toward day-to-day survival. You'll need one that addresses the essential skills for true nourishment of the human spirit. Living through the end of the world isn't worth a damn unless you can enjoy yourself in any way you want. (Except, of course, for anything having to do with abuse. We could never condone such things. At least the publisher's lawyers say we can't.)

PERMUTED
PRESS